Andrew Stevenson S.S.C. is a practising solicitor advocate at Waddell and Mackintosh, Troon. He has undertaken many hundreds of proofs across Scotland since 1992 in virtually all areas of litigation and has long experience of acting as a commissioner to recover evidence in sheriff court actions both civil and criminal. Andrew is a former President of the Glasgow Bar Association and he is currently Secretary of the Scottish Law Agents' Society. He is also a committee member of the Society of Solicitor Advocates. Andrew has written extensively on civil procedure and gives seminars on proofs and litigation. He is a contributor to *Greens Litigation Styles*. He is a regular columnist for *The Scotsman* and is a vice convenor of the Discipline Tribunal of the Church of Scotland. He is the author of *Style Writs for the Sheriff Court,* Bloomsbury 2023.

A Practical Guide to Conducting a Sheriff Court Proof

A Practical Guide to Conducting a Sheriff Court Proof

Andrew Stevenson

Law Brief Publishing

Published 2023 by Law Brief Publishing, an imprint of Law Brief Publishing Ltd
30 The Parks
Minehead
Somerset
TA24 8BT

www.lawbriefpublishing.com

Paperback: 978-1-916698-25-3

PREFACE

We practitioners all want to do the best for our clients, to be properly remunerated within a reasonable period and to minimize stress, complaints and an erosion of our leisure time. This book is from the coalface of the proof courts, the product of over thirty years' experience of encountering and only sometimes avoiding the pitfalls, snares and tripping hazards that bedevil the path of virtually every litigation. It is always better for a reader to learn from the mistakes of the author than from his or her own blunders, and if this guide can help any of my colleagues to avoid making an error I will consider it to have been a success.

A courteous and collegiate approach is vital to the future wellbeing of our profession. Generally, lawyers are not a breed fondly regarded by the public and there are enough ill-wishers out there without us making life difficult for each other.

It takes six years of education and training to produce a lawyer who is ready to undertake a proof in the Scottish courts. Experience then builds confidence. The notion that "user-friendly" procedure and shrieval intervention will enable unskilled and unexperienced litigants to conduct litigation without disadvantage to themselves and others is specious, and likely to result in instances of unfairness, extra cost and delay.

The book is dedicated to the countless hardworking and diligent civil court lawyers who I have met over the years, primarily in Glasgow Sheriff Court, who undertake an often thankless task for often demanding clients in the most challenging circumstances. Most are extremely modest and many are self-doubting, averse to seeking publicity or celebrity. Nonetheless, these self-effacing practitioners are the backbone of our civil justice system, and deserve to be appreciated, supported and valued.

The law is stated as at 1st November 2023.

Andrew Stevenson S.S.C., Solicitor Advocate
November 2023

CONTENTS

CHAPTER 1

INTRODUCTION

This book is intended to be a practical guide to conducting a proof in the sheriff court. The one unknown at present is the long-term legacy of Covid. It was far from clear in the chaos of 2020 whether the emergency measures put in place would be lifted once the pandemic was over or whether many of those provisions would remain in place.

It was always competent to use live video links to call witnesses but it was exceptional. That changed in 2020. The first reported hybrid proof, post-Covid may be *ER v CD* Perth Sheriff Court, 2nd September 2020, where the proof was "conducted using a combination of social distancing and video links to the Defender". At the time this was seen as something of a novelty; but that manner of conducting a proof is not seen as unusual at all now.

There is undoubtedly a strong desire amongst those who decide how litigation is conducted to maximise the use of remote court appearances. As far as proofs are concerned, having conducted plenty in person and remotely, and having sat as a tribunal member to hear witnesses both physically and via a screen, my view is that the latter is a second-rate method of gathering and assessing evidence, a view that I know is shared by many sheriffs. It is to be hoped that remote proofs will once again be exceptional. Conducting a proof over computer screens hampers the decision maker's ability to discern subtle body language that conveys confidence, deceit etc. The argument is advanced that a remote proof saves time and money. True, but it is cheap for a reason.

There has been much consultation on the future of proofs, and whether they should be remote or not. A Scottish Government Consultation on

Covid Recovery; Public Health, Services and Justice System Reform Paper stated that in the context of Covid emergency legislation an "unprecedented opportunity therefore exists to re-imagine public services" (including justice) and that we will "become a digital nation".

Related to that there was a now closed consultation by the Scottish Civil Justice Council where there was the suggestion that new rules would take proofs out of the open courtroom except where there was a significant issue of credibility.

The Response by the Society of Solicitor Advocates dated 8th November 2021 took the view that where there are issues of credibility it is crucial that the sheriff have the best possible opportunity to make an accurate assessment, and this requires that the sheriff be in proximity to the witness. The Response recommended that all other proofs be heard in person too. For one thing, it is often impossible to predict when an issue of credibility or reliability will arise.

Hearing a proof in open court means that it is treated by the participants with the full gravity that it deserves. This was lacking in a remote proof conducted by me in 2022 in which a witness gave evidence from the driver's seat of his works van, the steering wheel and dangling air freshener clearly visible from the camera of his mobile phone perched on the dashboard.

CHAPTER 2

RISK MANAGEMENT

For any practitioner, the single most important consideration is protection against the hazards that are inherent in running any proof. Conducting a proof is a risky business, and clients are all too ready to contact the Scottish Legal Complaints Commission to complain that it is their lawyer's fault that they lost their case. However, if you keep self-preservation as your priority you will also usually (but not always) serve your client's interests too.

Turning up in court and running a proof should be the relatively straightforward stage. The difficult and the tedious part is the preparation, but it is this that most helps in your efforts to minimise risks.

Identifying Conflicts of Interest is an essential element of risk management. Doing so helps locate where risks lie and where grievances might arise. These interests can usefully be regarded under the headings which correlate to the different capacities under which the solicitor is acting in the context of a proof. Lawyers are good are envisaging and taking precautions against worst case scenarios that might face their clients, whether that be in carrying out due diligence in conveyancing or lodging a caveat at court, but too often fail to apply the same pessimistic cynicism when it comes to covering their own backs.

CHAPTER 3

THE CAPACITIES IN WHICH YOU ARE ACTING

In preparing for and conducting a proof you are always acting in at least two of several legal capacities simultaneously;

1) You are always an officer of the court.

2) You may be a direct agent for one of the litigants.

3) You may be conducting the proof as a sub-contractor for another solicitor who is acting for the litigant.

4) Unless you are in the unusual position of acting as *amicus curiae* or you are undertaking the work *pro bono* you are a renumerated employee or self-employed.

5) You may be a recipient of funding from the Scottish Legal Aid Board, an insurance company or a trade union.

6) You are the colleague of the solicitor on the other side (if there is one) and even if the opponent is a party litigant or is represented by an unqualified person (which is now permissible under the Ordinary Cause Rules) you have a duty to that person to act fairly and candidly.

Each of these capacities has its own interests, and these interests can conflict. Indeed, in 3) above there is a potential conflict within that one capacity.

Going back to the need to protect yourself against risk, you can see that these capacities suggest and indicate where the risks lie and who is likely to complain. Consider them in order, asking that unsettling but crucial question, who is likely to complain about you and why?

CHAPTER 4

OFFICER OF THE COURT

This term derives from the fact that solicitors are appointed by the Court of Session, not by the government. Incidentally, if a sheriff ever reminds you that you are an officer of the court it is a bad sign, just as if a sheriff reminds a witness that he is under oath.

As regards one's duty to the court Rule B1.13.1 of the Law Society of Scotland Practice Rules 2011 states that; "You must never knowingly give false or misleading information to the court. You must maintain due respect and courtesy towards the court while honourably pursuing the interests of your clients." The latter part of this latter sentence recognises there is another capacity in which the solicitor acts, namely as agent for a client. However, the situation is more nuanced than may initially be apparent.

Breaching a duty arising from one's status as an officer of the court could in theory give rise to a complaint by the court itself. Section 2 of the Legal Profession and Legal Aid (Scotland) Act 2007 allows "any judge (including a sheriff)" to make a complaint to the SLCC. In practice, such a complaint is more likely to be threatened than made. What is more problematic is reputational damage to the solicitor as a result of uncomplimentary comments made by the court. Sometimes these make their way into reported case decisions. This looks bad. It should be avoided at all costs. Case reports often avoid naming and thereby embarrassing a sheriff who has "misdirected himself" or "fallen into error" to use another euphemism or similarly made himself vulnerable to being overturned, but they are not nearly as protective of solicitors.

As an officer of the court as well as never "knowingly" giving misinformation to the court you must not do so recklessly or carelessly. So if you are asked a question by the sheriff and you do not know the answer never guess. That can end in tears.

Knowingly in the context of a proof is allowing evidence or information that you know is false to be led. So if in a divorce case your client informs you of the existence of an asset or an income stream that he does not want his wife or the court to know about it you cannot facilitate or turn a blind eye to his endeavours to mislead the court into thinking that the asset or income does not exist by, for example, his failing to declare it on the disclosure Form F13A.

If, as once happened to me, a witness of your client admits to you, his guilty conscience having compelled him to do so, that he has lied during a proof you need to disclose this to the court. Doing nothing makes you an accessory to the deceit.

Although you cannot knowingly or carelessly mislead a court by allowing false evidence or information to be put before it, this does not mean that you are expected to believe everything your client tells you. In fact, it is far healthier not to do so but to keep an open mind instead. One of the hallmarks of a good lawyer is to put himself into the shoes of the opponent and to think about how he would conduct the litigation if Destiny had placed him in the opposing corner. (A similar approach is to conjure up the image of the proof calling in a week's time. This focusses the mind on the most urgent preparations still be to done.)

You are perfectly entitled to lead evidence which you personally believe to be a pack of lies; as long as the client has not *told* you that it is a pack of lies. Equally, there is absolutely nothing unethical in asking the court to do something that you personally think would be disastrous; such as moving the sheriff to award child contact to a convicted abuser. If you feel that you cannot stomach doing this, which would be perfectly understandable, do not act; there are plenty of other lawyers out there who will.

Never assume that your client is being truthful. Instances arise all the time where the only conclusion is that someone is lying.

If you are asked to present a hopeless case or try to prove a case that you personally think is nonsense do not say "I don't believe you" but "I am concerned that the court will not believe you." Then say why. Your own opinion as to somebody's credibility or reliability is irrelevant. It does not matter what you think, what matters is your assessment of what the sheriff is likely to think.

Being an officer of the court does not mean that you have to avoid standing up to a sheriff. Remember that if sheriffs were infallible there would be no need for the Sheriff Appeal Court. There are plenty of seminars and talks with titles such as "How not to annoy your sheriff". My view of this is that there is nothing wrong *per se* with annoying a sheriff. In general, sheriffs should not be getting angry. Compared to many in this world they do not really have a great deal to get angry about. A sheriff is paid £143,095 *per annum,* hears cases between 10am and 4pm and has generous holidays and a good pension.

The best sheriffs are cool, calm and collected. It is not your job not to annoy a sheriff. Whether it is wrong to do it depends on why the sheriff is getting annoyed. So if the sheriff is annoyed because you are asking daft questions, or bullying a witness, that is fair enough.

If, on the other hand, if you are trying to conduct a proof, you want to call a witness, the sheriff appears to have made up his mind already and is getting annoyed because you carry on regardless, that is not fair enough. You might need to get that evidence in to support an appeal.

As an adjunct to the adage that you should never interrupt an enemy who is making a mistake, it can be an effective tactic not to object to the opposing solicitor who is annoying the sheriff. Do not take this too far, however, or you will attract anger for not objecting.

The Law Society Practice Rule B1.13, headed "Relations with the Courts" says, amongst other things that "You must maintain due respect and courtesy towards the court while honourably pursuing the interests of your client."

The Practice Rules pertaining to solicitor advocates say (at C4.4.19) that "you must be fearless in defending your client's interests, regardless of the consequences to yourself (including, if necessary, incurring the displeasure of the bench.)" That enjoinder to be fearless should apply, and I think that it does apply, to solicitors generally.

Incidentally, as an officer of the court you must cite caselaw that is relevant even if it does not help your case (in which scenario you must try to differentiate the facts of the case from your own). This obligation is not one which burdens;

Party litigants

They are not "officers of the court", of course, and they are not bound by any practice rules. One should never generalise, nor underestimate them. Some can be difficult to deal with, belligerent and paying little or no attention to rules or etiquette. Some can be articulate, persuasive and well prepared. You will find that they get away with many defaults but will object to yours more than another lawyer would do. To be fair, they often see the answer to the question "Are you objecting to the production, lodged one day late?" as being "Sure, why wouldn't I?". After all, they view the sole purpose of being there as to win the case, they care not about falling out with lawyers and know not that the sheriff is almost certain to repel their objection.

Check to see whether they have lodged anything (list of witnesses, productions, statements, letters to the judge etc) because you cannot assume that they will have intimated anything. Turning up to find page after page of productions or a ten-page email explaining their position just wastes time.

CHAPTER 5

ACTING AS DIRECT AGENT FOR A LITIGANT

The most dangerous source of complaints is one's own client. This is nothing new. The Roman historian, Ammianus Marcellinus, circa 400 A.D., said that almost every litigant thinks that it is the fault of his advocate if he loses his case, despite the fact that this can occur due to any one of a thousand accidents. It is always the advocate, not the weakness of the case or, frequently, the court's partiality, that brings about the outcome, and the client's anger is focussed only on him.

Statistically, there are roughly as many losers in winners in the sheriff court. It is not an exactly equal split because in some cases there is a plurality of pursuers or of defenders or of both, and in many cases there is mixed success. But broadly speaking one can safely say that a large proportion of clients lose their case, and that a large proportion of them will manifest the unfortunate and, from the lawyer's perspective, the dangerous characteristic identified by Ammianus Marcellinus 1600 years ago. Incidentally, Ammianus' "thousand accidents" is mirrored in a wonderful dictum by temporary Judge Reid Q.C. in *Susan McNeish v Advocate General* 2004;

> *"Litigation is a risky business. For one reason or another, it rarely goes according to plan."*

This all points to the fact that mishaps and risks are endemic in court actions. Having said that, there is a relatively small (but very broad) number of issues about which a client will complain. Here is another quote, this time by the English philosopher Jeremy Bentham (1748 – 1832);

> *"Vexation, delay and expense are the burthens inseparably attendant on judicial procedure."*

This remark well encapsulates the three areas that will generate a complaint by the client. It does not matter what kind of case it is, a client is likely to be aggrieved about three things; a bad outcome, delay and cost. It has always been like that. What is new is that we have the SLCC, a compensation culture, an erosion of respect for professional people and the fact that clients seem increasingly unwilling to accept that the reason they may have lost a case is that the sheriff simply did not believe them.

Significantly, these three factors signify areas over which the solicitor has limited control. The outcome of a proof is ultimately a matter for the court. Delay is largely due to the timetabling laid down by the sheriff or the sheriff clerk. Frequently it is determined by how busy the court happens to be with other business. Cost is often the result of the actions of the other party or his agent. For example, in general terms it is up to the other side to decide how many productions to lodge, how many witnesses to call, how long to take in questioning them and in cross examining your witnesses. In this way litigation differs from other areas of work such as most private client business where, for example, it is possible to quote £125 plus VAT to prepare a will. Defended litigation defies this kind of prospective assessment of fees, to clients' frustration.

Before addressing these three areas let us consider;

<u>The scope of your authority as agent</u>

Remember that you can act only on your client's instructions. You can advise but your client doesn't have to follow your advice; but it isn't a *quid pro quo*; you <u>have</u> to follow his instructions.

Problems can arise where your client thinks that he is better qualified than you in how to conduct a proof. Common issues are;

i. The client wants to give evidence or wants to call someone else to give evidence when you advise against it.

ii. He wants to lodge a production and you do not.

iii. He wants you to ask a particular question of a witness when you think that to do so would be a bad idea.

These are all examples of adducing evidence that your client thinks will help his case, but where you disagree.

In my view although you are an agent acting on instructions you cannot do your job properly if you cannot exercise your professional judgment without the client persistently challenging it. If the client is going to do that he clearly lacks trust in your professionalism and you should politely suggest that he gets another lawyer or does the job himself.

In any case that is heading towards a proof you should always make it clear to the client that you need the freedom to make judgements and decisions on your feet. There simply will not be the opportunity for you to get instructions on every question that you put during examination of a witness, for example. Such micromanagement by the client would be unworkable and unreasonable.

Keep a detailed file note that you have made this clear to the client and that he understands and consents to that position.

Instructions can be withdrawn at any time and without any warning or explanation (so you have to get funding up front). You can be sacked at any time; but it feels much worse if you then have to chase payment of fees.

Equally, you can decline to act for someone; one of the few advantages that our profession has over that of teachers or NHS doctors is that we can choose not to take on a case. So, if you feel uncomfortable, e.g. if somebody is trying to lead you into behaving unethically, you can always decline to act or withdraw from acting; indeed, that may be the only course that you should take. The earlier that you do that the better. You do have to be careful about prejudicing the client (e.g. withdrawing the day before a proof) and, I realise, that if you are employed you may feel pressurised into continuing to act.

Where you act directly for a litigant and the proof does go ahead there can be tensions and conflicts, between how you minimise the risks of complaint and how best to promote your client's interests, reconciling the factors of cost and delay. It is a balancing exercise; there will almost always be more evidence out there than your client leads, wherever you choose to draw the line. The best advice to a client might well be to lead less evidence that he has, in order to minimise the expense and delay of a proof if further time is necessary. But that carries risks. If your client loses he may later claim that you had given bad advice to refrain from calling a witness whose evidence, it may be said, would have turned the case in favour of the client. This has happened to me. It led to a complaint to the SLCC. The fact that it failed dismally was little consolation for all the time and energy I had to waste answering it.

In acting directly for a litigant you do so under the common law principle that an agent for a disclosed principal is not personally liable for that principal's debts. However, there are some extremely important exceptions to the application of this principle, and you may find yourself undertaking some steps which are not covered by the common law protection already mentioned. The most significant of these is where there is personal liability to third parties to meet outlays associated with the proof.

CHAPTER 6

ACTING AS AN AGENT FOR ANOTHER SOLICITOR

This is the third of the capacities noted above. In this situation you are required to protect the interests of the instructing agents and also their client even although you have no direct contract with the latter. There are some advantages in acting for another solicitor. It shouldn't be a problem getting paid. Section 30 of the Solicitors (Scotland) Act 1980 states that a solicitor who employs another solicitor to do work – such as conducting a proof – is liable for his fees and outlays unless he expressly disclaims any such liability (something I have never seen done).

So this is a statutory exception to the rule that an agent for a disclosed principal has no personal liability.

If you are running a proof for somebody else you shouldn't really have any responsibility with funding generally. It is not your job to pay the shorthand writer or witnesses.

Acting for another solicitor can give rise to conflicts; e.g. let us say that a proof is going badly because the principal agent's written pleadings are rubbish or the principal agent has failed to call an important witness or lodge an important document. You might want to try to get the proof halted so that consideration can be given to amending, or trying to get hold of the person whose evidence is required or lodging a production late. But there could well be adverse consequences in expenses if you do that. In addition, you are drawing the client's attention to an omission by the principal agent; the principal agent might not want you to do that. The best course, if possible, is to get a short adjournment, tell the court and client that you need to discuss a matter with the principal agent (do not elaborate) and go and phone them and see what they want to do; i.e. let them take the decision and responsibility.

One disadvantage is that you might never have met the client until the morning of the proof itself. Civil agency practitioners may well encounter other challenges which may make some of the advice in this book seem like a counsel of perfection. Such lawyers may well not have the luxury of being able to spend many hours preparing for a proof; if one is conducting a proof having been handed the papers the evening before you simply will not have had time to do the preparation that you would ideally want to have done. Principal agents will sometimes wait until the eleventh hour to deliver papers in the hope that the case will settle and that they will be able to avoid paying the agency solicitor to undertake preparation. Agency solicitors should ensure that they receive the paperwork as early as possible.

Another precaution that the local agent should insist upon is that the client knows that the principal agent will not be conducting the proof. Even better, you should meet with the client in advance of the day of the proof itself or at the very least have a telephone discussion. It is not a good start to be met with the questions "Where's Mr Swindell?" or "Who the blazes are you?" Even if you are a better lawyer than Mr Swindell, the client can feel uninformed and disrespected.

Preparing well in advance and speaking to witnesses yourself in advance of the proof minimizes the risk of a conflict of interest arising on the day where, for example a witness gives evidence at odds with his precognition; that causes problems and you are left trying to smooth it over without getting your instructing agent into an argument with the client about what the precognosee actually said. Another recommendation is that unless they are going to be in the court building themselves make sure that you have a line of communication to the instructing agent so that if anything goes awry you can advise them and let them take the decision on what to do about it. So if a witness materially deviates from her precognition or a vital piece of evidence is missing my view is that it should be the instructing agent's call as to what should be done about it.

Remember that you always have to cover your own back. Remember too that if you take a major decision off your own bat you could be in a conflict with the principal agent. So where a proof is going wrong there are various options; If there is a Tender or Pursuer's Offer you might think that it should be accepted. You might think that there needs to be a motion made to amend. You might think that somebody else needs to be cited as a witness or a document needs to be lodged. My view is; make it the principal agent's decision. The nuclear option may be to try to get the proof discharged. I have never had to do this but I have seen agents asking to speak to the sheriff in chambers and talking about withdrawing from acting. It is never a good look.

Again, prepare well in advance and try to spot potential problems and address them. Sometimes, though, you just have to think quickly and hope for some luck. I conducted a road traffic accident proof in Hamilton where a collision had occurred on a roundabout in East Kilbride. The pursuer was not from EK and the productions lodged on his behalf showed a particular roundabout. It was not the same as the roundabout shown in the photographs lodged by the defender. I didn't have time to get to the bottom of this before arriving at court. The pursuer was pleasant, but not the sharpest tool in the box. I was able to speak to him and he came to realize that the roundabout where the accident had happened was indeed the one shown in the opponent's photographs. The fault there lay with the pursuer. What I did there was run the proof but ignore the pursuer's photographs, referring him to the defender's. That actually worked. I was expecting the defender's solicitor to ask him; why did you lodge photographs of a random roundabout where the accident did not occur? But he did not. So that is an example of smoothing away any bad feeling or conflict between the instructing agent and their client. Some of these conflicts are unavoidable. Generally, they are down to bad communication. To minimize the risk, ensure that you feel comfortable taking the instructions. You have to be able to trust the instructing agent not to give you a hospital pass. Prepare as early as possible, and insist on getting the papers as soon as possible. If you can, speak yourself to the key witnesses in advance (i.e. not on the day) and check that the precognitions are consistent with the pleadings. That way, if they are not, you can prepare your questions in such a way as not to look daft and, if necessary, the opportunity is there to amend and hopefully to preserve the proof. Unless they are going to be at the court themselves make sure that you have a line of communication to the instructing agent so that if anything goes badly wrong you can advise them and let them take the decision on what to do about it.

It is more important to avoid conflicts of interest as opposed to analysing those that arise.

The first thing is to ensure that you and the instructing agent are as one as regards the advice given to the client. This includes managing client expectations.

That applies too as regards settlement. If you tell the client on the day that an offer of £10,000 should be accepted and the principal agent has already advised him not to take less than £15,000 you can see that the client might be confused and think that somebody is incompetent.

A tricky conflict of interest is where you turn up at court to conduct a proof and it soon becomes apparent to you that the instructing agents haven't done something that they ought to have done, such as lodge a production on time.

In my view you have a duty to look after your instructing agents interests by not exposing them needlessly to a risk of complaint or criticism by their client. On the other hand you have a duty to be straight and open and candid with their client.

It could be that there is not actually much of a conflict; in the example of the late production, both the client and the instructing agents have the same interest, namely getting the production in late. The conflict has more of a potential nature, e.g. if there is an inadequacy or blunder in the pleadings or in precognitions or there is a failure to produce sufficient evidence.

None of the foregoing is to suggest that you should avoid exercising initiative or judgment of your own. Sometimes you have to think on your feet and be pragmatic. And since you are the man or woman on the ground if a conflict does arise later between yourself and the instructing agent you can say that you were there, the instructing agent was not, events were moving and you had to deal with the situation as it was; "Litigation is a risky business. For one reason or another it rarely goes according to plan."

CHAPTER 7

ACTING AS AN EMPLOYEE

You have to ensure that you are not going to land your employers with a bill which they are unable to pay without resorting to using their own money. In other words, try to make sure that you have adequate funding up front to run a proof. This is vitally important. Going into court to conduct a proof is expensive. But, more importantly, it can be expensive for your employer personally. (This all applies if you are a self-employed solicitor too). You have to endeavor to guarantee that you get paid, and to make a profit from doing the work; there is absolutely no point in conducting a proof if you are going to lose money.

Do not end up being left having to shell out when you are not in funds to cover that outlays. Many of the costs involved in running a proof are the personal responsibility of the solicitor. So as well as all your other responsibilities you are lumbered with being guarantor for the client's debts. There may be public policy reasons behind this; it brings the reputation of the courts into disrepute if witnesses and others don't have the ability to get their costs from the lawyer who compelled them to go to court. There are certainly four groups of people that you are personally liable to pay; shorthand writers, witnesses whom you cite, sheriff officers and counsel. In addition, you are probably personally liable for the sheriff's clerk's fees.

In theory, you could have a proof under Ordinary Procedure where you will not face all these risks;

i) The court may dispense with the attendance of a shorthand writer if the parties agree; *Macphail* 16.32, referring to OCR

29.18(1) That, incidentally, is risky if you have to appeal, because there will be no record of the evidence other than the sheriff's own notes.

ii) You may not have cited any witnesses. They might have attended voluntarily, or your client might be the only witness or you may have no witnesses at all and you simply cross examine the opponent's witnesses.

iii) You may not have instructed sheriff officers to cite witnesses. You usually would not and if you do have to do so it calls into question how helpful such a reluctant witness might actually be.

iv) You may not have instructed counsel. Incidentally, bear in mind that counsel is never liable to meet any outlays.

So let us look at shorthand writers and witnesses in the context of their chasing you for money, suing you or going off to the SLCC;

A) Shorthand writers

You do not need to worry about shorthand writers in proofs in Edinburgh Sheriff Court. You might in Summary Applications. You do in Ordinary Causes.

The provisions that matter here are;

OCR 29.18 which says that the shorthand writer's fees are payable in the first instance by the parties equally but also that "The solicitors for the parties shall be personally liable for the fees". So you are having to underwrite personally that the shorthand writer will get paid.

This is another exception to the rule that an agent for a disclosed principal is not liable for the principal's debt. In relation to the Defender it is even more exceptional or radical because the Defender does not even have a contract with the shorthand writer; it is the pursuer who instructs him.

For proceedings raised after 29th April 2019 Chapter 7 of the 2019 Act of Sederunt governs the amount that is payable. That Act and its immediate predecessor, the Act of Sederunt (Fees of Witnesses and Shorthand Writers in the Sheriff Court) 1992 are virtually the same in how they quantify these outlays.

Witnesses are covered in Chapter 7.1 and Schedule 6 and shorthand writers in Chapter 7.2 and Schedule 7.

The sum that you could be personally liable to pay a shorthand writer is substantial.

Both the 1992 and the 2019 Acts of Sederunt provide for an attendance fee, expressed as an hourly amount subject to a daily minimum which is the equivalent of about four hours. The figures are roughly £44 and £177 exclusive of any VAT.

Secondly, there is provision for a cancellation fee. Nothing is due if the shorthand writer is cancelled more than 21 days before, and the full daily fee is due if the cancellation takes place after 4pm the day before. This begs the question of why (apart from saving the cost of reimbursing travelling expenses) one would bother cancelling at all after 4pm, particularly if there is a risk, however remote, that the proof will proceed. Between these limits 75% is payable, ie about £132; at current rates.

There is a subsistence allowance and copying charge. In addition, shorthand writers invariably request a booking fee. This is essentially a deposit, retained if the proof does not proceed or deducted from the final bill if it does. This is not unreasonable, and it is perhaps surprising that it is not officially sanctioned. There is a reference in the first edition (1988) of *Macphail*, at 16.34. to a practice (probably now redundant) of refunding the fee if the proof is discharged more than 21 days in advance

But most significantly, there is extension of the shorthand notes. (£7.25 per sheet; that's under both the 1992 and the 2019 Acts of Sederunt). This just means that the notes are typed out. Victorian legislation once required a shorthand writer to extend the notes, but now whether this is done or not is now a decision entirely for the court. This is where the greatest potential cost lies. One prominent shorthand writers' firm estimates that an hour's oral evidence equates to 40 sheets, ie £290 per hour. So a five hour proof would generate a standard fee of £1450. Where the shorthand writer is VAT registered (and not all of them are) this cost is inflated to £1740. One can see why agents will generally resist a proposal by the sheriff for an extension of the shorthand notes.

There is the risk of a shorthand writer costing you (personally) a thousand pounds, ie your half of the bill in the event of the sheriff ordering the extension of the notes.

It is good practice to get a thousand pounds per day from a private client just to cover that potential liability.

B) <u>Witness who is cited by the solicitor</u>

Where Covid Rules have applied there has been a significant effect in relation to witnesses insofar as suspending the need for physical attendance and making provision for attendance by remote means. Witness expenses were less, due to the absence of travelling and subsistence costs.

In any event, you have to be extremely careful and to anticipate the witness sending you an astronomical bill for having been in court. He might send you a bill for the time he claims to have spent reading over papers. And naturally, he's going to look to you for payment before he starts chasing the client.

Assuming that your client wins, and is granted an award of expenses, the 2019 and the 1992 Acts of Sederunt cap at £400 plus VAT per day the amount that he is able to recover from the opponent, to cover his liability to pay each of his own witnesses in terms of their financial loss (excluding travel and subsistence costs; worth bearing in mind if the witness has to come from hundreds of miles away.) The exception is for skilled witnesses, where there is no cap; the limit is whatever the auditor thinks is reasonable.

So if the witness loses earnings of £600 to attend court under a citation from you, and claims that money, your client is going to be left with £200 that he cannot claim back from the opponent.

The key to dealing with this is to discuss the issue of costs with your client's witnesses in advance. Naturally, people do not like going to court to give evidence. And if they can put you off citing them by quoting a massive bill they might feel tempted to do that. But, they cannot actually do that. It would be detrimental to the administration of justice if that were permissible. It is not. Witnesses have to be able to justify and vouch their actual costs and they have to mitigate those.

One way of minimising witness expenses (and putting them in a better frame of mind) is to make arrangements to have your witnesses ready at the end of a phone line. So they can get on with work in the office. This is an extremely common practice, particularly in relation to professional or expert witnesses.

C) <u>Sheriff Officers</u>

The courts have found that despite the law protecting an agent from liability for the debt of a disclosed principal such liability can arise through custom. This has been held to cover sheriff officers; *Stirling Park and Co v Digby Brown* 1996 SLT (Sh Ct) 17.

D) Personal liability for counsel's fees.

Any solicitor who instructs counsel "accepts a professional obligation to pay counsel's fees in accordance with the scheme" (Faculty of Advocates Scheme for the Accounting for and Recovery of Counsel's Fees August 2020.). The Scheme reiterates the law that "Counsel does not enter into any contractual relationship with the instructing person or the lay client."

E) The Sheriff Clerk's Fees

By contrast to the position regarding witnesses and shorthand writers there is no explicit rule that makes you personally liable for these costs. There is, however, *AB v CD (1843) 6 D 95,* a 180-year old Court of Session case referred to in *McLaren* and *Macphail.* Taken together with years of habit and practice, and the certainty that the sheriff clerk will be looking to you to pay court fees, you should assume that you are personally liable. These costs can be substantial; a sheriff court Ordinary Cause proceeding to a two-day proof will cost a pursuer almost £800. And if the fees are not paid the case will run into logistical problems, such as that you might never get the clerk to call the case for proof.

The one saving grace is that sheriff court proofs are charged at the rate of £251 per day, payable by the pursuer only. By contrast, in the Court of Session a judge's time is charged at £884 per hour. This is charged at £221 per half hour, payable both by the pursuer and also separately by the defender.

There is a grey area regarding;

1) Interpreters. As with shorthand writers these are not provided by the court in civil proceedings and they take the oath *de fidele administrationis* but there is no rule making a solicitor personally liable for their fees.

2) Experts instructed but not cited. My view is that in general you are not personally liable. But there could be circumstances where you are liable, by implied contract. In *Wight Chiropractic Clinic Ltd v Corries (Scotland) Solicitors*, 12th October 2005, reported on the SCTS Website, a cited witness was paid normally as an employee; the entity which suffered loss was his employer, which had not been cited, but which sued the solicitors. Bear in mind too that whilst you may have a defence in law you do not want the creditor running off and making a complaint about you to the SLCC.

It is worth observing that niceties over the legal basis on which there is personal liability or not are going to avail you little if there is a complaint to the SLCC. Also, who really wants the risk, publicity and inconvenience of being the defender in a test case over whether, for example, personal liability attaches to solicitors for the fees of interpreters?

CHAPTER 8

RECIPIENT OF THIRD-PARTY FUNDING

Here, you are being paid by somebody other than the client. I mean the sort of third party that would customarily provide funding rather than your client's parents or a philanthropic stranger (which can give rise to a whole different set of issues, such as whether such a funder could be regarded as *dominis litis* and therefore face an award against him if the funded party loses).

Conventional funding by an institution requires you to have regard to the costs to and the restrictions imposed by the third-party funder.

Legal Aid

The risk of being piggy in the middle is much more in a case when your client is an "assisted person" (the term of someone in receipt of legal aid.) Because you cannot get the money up front, you are left having to pay out to witnesses, experts, the shorthand writer and so on in the hope that you will get reimbursed by the Board later down the line. All that you can do is cross your fingers, make sure that you have sanction and that your case cost ceiling is likely to be enough. But it is risky. Nobody will charge less because your client has legal aid. Certainly, you will not have to worry about court fees (your client is exempt) but that is about the only good point about having legal aid.

Note that if you are acting for an assisted person you have duties under Regulation 24 of the Civil Legal Aid (Scotland) Regulations 2002; headed "Duty to report abuse of legal aid". If you have reason to believe that the assisted person has unreasonably required the cause to be continued you have to tell the Board; and that duty over-rides any agent-client privilege of confidentiality. So private clients can waste their own money, assisted persons are not allowed to waste public money.

If you choose to conduct a proof under legal aid you will be paid less than half the amount you would have received had the client been paying privately, and you will have to maintain exactly the same standards and face the same risks of complaint. In addition, you will have an extra layer of administration and you will not have the security of having funding up front to meet outlays.

Whether your firm is benevolent enough to offer legal aid or not you have to know a bit about how this affects expenses of a litigation, including a proof. So if your client's opponent has legal aid you need to warn your client about the risks that creates. Because, even if the assisted person loses it is likely that your client will not be able to get expenses from him. This is because in terms of Section 18 of the 1986 Act the assisted person is entitled to ask the court to modify any liability in expenses to a lower figure than he would require to pay if he were not in receipt of legal aid, or to nil. And that motion will almost certainly be granted. In my experience it will not be granted only if the assisted person has behaved dishonestly.

The last of the capacities mentioned was colleague of the opposing solicitor. Remember that clients come and go and that solicitors have long memories. Getting one over on another solicitor might taste sweet at the time, but beware karma in the long term. This profession is meant to be collegiate.

CHAPTER 9

RISK MANAGEMENT: HOW TO AVOID HAVING TO CONDUCT A PROOF

The most emphatic way of avoiding the risks of a proof is to avoid having one at all.

The Advantages of Settling

The great advantage of settlement is that you retain control and thereby minimise risk. You are not dependent on the goodwill, knowledge and discretion of a third party, the sheriff. Settlement is either judicial or extra-judicial, and it is often possible to try both simultaneously to get resolution without a proof at all.

From the perspective of self-protection it is always better to settle a case for a bird in the hand than to proceed to a proof in the hope of winning two in the bush. Assume that there is a payment action for £20,000. If you act for the pursuer and settle for, say, £15,000 then the client will get £15,000. If he had gone to proof he might have got more, but he might have got less, or nothing at all. If you settle the client will never know what would have happened if he had gone to proof and is unlikely to be able to complain about having had bad advice to settle for £15,000 because nobody can say what the alternative would have been. In an extreme case there could be a legitimate complaint; for example if you have a factory worker injured in an industrial accident and you advise him that the loss of his leg is worth £3000, and that he should settle for that figure. But in most cases, settlement is unlikely to result in the client complaining.

The same reasoning applies if you settle on behalf of a defender. This is how you can turn to your advantage the risks involved in going ahead with a proof. Virtually anybody can be persuaded of the benefits of settlement. Also, trying to settle a proof is always worth doing because if discussions fall through its easier to say to the client that he was left with no reasonable alternative but to go to proof.

However, never look desperate to settle.

Tenders and Pursuer's Offers

The other step to take if you can is to lodge a Tender, or a Pursuer's Offer; that is a method of trying to settle, and it is also a good way of putting pressure on your opponent.

A tender is accepted by lodging a Minute of Acceptance of Tender and it is withdrawn by lodging a Minute of Withdrawal of Tender. If you are undertaking a proof where a tender has been lodged, my advice if you are acting for the Pursuer is to keep a withdrawal of tender inside your file ready to be lodged if the proof seems to be going against the Defender. If you are for the Defender keep an acceptance of tender in your file for the same reasons. It is not unknown for parties' agents to get into a race in writing out a withdrawal and an acceptance of a tender so as to lodge it first.

Macphail 14.52 refers to a Tender lapsing by an important change of circumstances. You should never rely on having to argue that. Treat it as live unless its explicitly withdrawn or accepted.

In order to motivate lawyers to settle the Table of Fees is quite generous in remunerating settlement attempts. It must be emphasised, however, that being a solicitor puts you in a fiduciary position, so that you have to put the client's interests first. So it would be unethical and a breach of that duty to advise settlement on terms that you consider inadequate or unreasonable.

The Advantages of Preparation

If you want peace, you should prepare for war according to the Roman historian Vegetius, circa 400 A.D. (around the same time as Ammianus Marcellinus, incidentally)

Early preparation is vital to nip in the bud that which might otherwise swell into a problem leading to a complaint.

Some solicitors gain a reputation for always settling actions. Do not be one of them. If you are involved in court work in any way you should try to conduct a proof at least now and again so that you appreciate what is involved. Even if you think that a case is likely to settle, to get a good deal you really have to convince your opponent that you are going to proof.

Risk Management; How to maximise control over the conduct of a proof.

The best way of doing this is to maximise areas of agreement so that the proof is restricted to those parts of the case that are in dispute. A good example is in relation to a road traffic accident. There are two components to such a case, namely liability and quantum. See below.

Notices to Admit

These are wonderful, and should be used a lot. You get paid for lodging them, it forces you to prepare for the proof six weeks in advance and it shows the court that you've done your best to try to cut down the evidence. Another option is to draft a Minute of Agreement. Also, not a bad idea but it is ineffective unless and until you get it signed by both parties' agents. And this can be risky; if the other side procrastinates you can end up running out of time to lodge a Notice to Admit and without having a signed Minute.

CHAPTER 10

POINTS TO ATTEND TO WHEN THE PROOF DATE IS BEING ASSIGNED

Proofs are assigned at Options Hearings, Procedural Hearings, and callings of Summary Applications, and some opposed motions such as where a sist is recalled, or a Record is opened, amended and closed, or administratively where a motion is granted unopposed. Whatever the circumstances;

1. Witness availability

You need to check your witness availability and communicate that to the court before the proof is fixed. There is no point in getting 2nd August 2024 assigned if a key witness has already booked a holiday in Lanzarote on that date. Write to all your witnesses advising that the court will be fixing the proof date, to let you know their unsuitable dates, update you as to new unsuitable dates and make it clear that you will assume that any date is suitable unless you are told otherwise. Then cite the witnesses as soon as possible after the proof date is fixed. This way, if someone says that he cannot attend you cannot be blamed for or expected to meet the expenses of the discharge of the proof.

2. Vulnerable Witnesses

The rules of court are full of references to vulnerable witnesses. The sheriff is supposed to enquire as to whether any proposed witnesses are vulnerable and citation forms advise that the witness who considers herself to be vulnerable they should tell the solicitor who has cited her. This seldom happens.

You should approach this matter pragmatically and as early as possible, so that appropriate arrangements can be made. In my experience sheriffs are accommodating about this. In a proof in Dunoon where one of the witnesses was a wheelchair user, we heard her evidence in the sheriff clerk's office. The office is on the ground floor whereas the only courtroom is on the first floor, and there is no lift. I had a proof in Airdrie and the witness, who was also a wheelchair user sat in her wheelchair beside the witness box instead of trying to manoeuvre herself into it. Incidentally, if you have a disability you should make that known to the clerk as early as possible.

Elderly witnesses may wish to give evidence on commission.

3. Shorthand Writer and Interpreter

If the case is a Summary Application ascertain from the sheriff whether he wishes a shorthand writer to be in attendance. In Ordinary Causes the default requirement is that a shorthand writer must attend proofs, but the Ordinary Cause Rules do not apply to Summary Applications, where the matter is for the sheriff's discretion.

If you are the Pursuer's agent in an Ordinary Cause remember to instruct a shorthand writer. Even if it is the Defender who is leading, and even if the Pursuer has no witnesses, it is still the responsibility of the Pursuer to instruct the shorthand writer; O.C.R. 29.15. On the other hand, it is for the party who needs an interpreter, be that the Pursuer, Defender, Party Minuter or other, to arrange that.

4. Hearing parts of a proof separately

This can be sensible in terms of time and cost management. Hearing parts of a proof separately is specifically permitted under O.C.R. 29.6. Two scenarios where this might be prudent is in a personal injury case where you could have a proof on liability only and then (only if liability is established) you would have a proof on quantum.

Another is where there is a preliminary proof, ie where an issue is raised in the written pleadings which might bar the action from proceeding. Three leap to mind; firstly where there is a plea of no jurisdiction, secondly where the issue of bar is raised (time bar, personal bar etc) and thirdly where the pursuer's title is challenged. So if somebody is suing in a capacity and that is disputed, it makes sense to have a preliminary proof.

Another scenario where a separate proof is sensible is in a divorce action where there is a dispute over the date of separation. You need to know the relevant date before you start leading evidence about the parties' assets and debts as at that date.

Onus of Proof; Is the Defender to lead at the proof?

You are not expected to try to prove a negative. So, assume that somebody raises an action for repayment of a loan. If the defender denies getting a loan the onus would be on the pursuer to prove that she lent the money. If the defender admitted getting the loan but said that he had repaid it the onus would be on him to prove that he had repaid it. It would not be up to the lender to "prove a negative" that he did not get repayment of money admittedly lent. That would be silly.

"Leading at proof" means going first. I have seen instances where a Pursuer wants the Defender to lead at proof, because the onus is on the Defender to prove something significant. But generally it is far easier to lead than not. This is because you do not have to worry about putting in cross examination, something that you are going to be asking your own witnesses in chief later on.

To explain, if you are going second, the other side has already given its evidence, which means that it no longer has a chance to lead evidence contrary to yours. So if there is evidence that you want to adduce, and fairness demands that the other side be given the chance to lead proof of the contrary, you have to let them know that you are going to be leading that evidence; and it is generally not enough just to rely on the written pleadings. You have to put your anticipated evidence to the opponent's witnesses if it is fair and reasonable to suppose that they might have something to say about it. So you would say "We may hear evidence later than you and not my client drove through a red light; what would you say to that?"

The default position is that the pursuer leads, i.e. goes first. Some solicitors think that it is always advantageous to compel the opponent to lead. It is not. I have never understood why any agent would want to relinquish the advantages of going first. Bear in mind that the onus of proof is unaffected by whether the pursuer or the defender leads.

Assume that there is a contract where goods are supplied for a price of £6000 and the defence is that the goods were defective. Common sense would suggest that the defender lead because the dispute is not that goods were supplied or that the price was £6000 but that the pursuer is in breach; the onus of proving that lies on the defender. A good way of determining who has the onus of proof is to ask who would win if no evidence were led and the court had to rely solely on presumptions. Here, there is a presumption of regularity, which favours the pursuer.

Assuming that the Record makes it clear that the fact of supply and the price of the goods is undisputed the only purpose in the pursuer going into the witness box at all is to make himself available for cross examination. Examination in chief of the pursuer need be restricted to asking him his name, age, address and occupation and to put a token point to him such as "It is not disputed that on 3rd September 2022 you and the defender, Mr Barnes, agreed that you would supply him with 1000kg of red pine decking for a price of £6000 and that you delivered that material on 5th October 2022". The witness would answer "Yes" and that would be the end of examination in chief.

By the way, although this is a blatantly leading question it does not elicit any evidence of anything in dispute and is therefore unobjectionable. A leading question is one which is designed to elicit a specific answer that the questioner is looking for. Such questions are normally objectionable; even if they are not objected to they will merely elicit evidence of doubtful weight.

It might be asked why there is any point in the pursuer giving evidence at all here. The reason is *Davidson v Duncan* 1981 (Session Cases) 83 In that case the Inner House held that where a defender has led no evidence only the most favourable inferences should be drawn from the pursuer's evidence. That was an action of count reckoning and payment following the dissolution of a partnership. In other types of case this may actually be quite an odd proposition; I conducted a proof on quantum in which I led no evidence, cross examining the pursuer's accountant, and I was successful.

Going back to the illustration provided, before Mr Barnes' lawyer can lead him and his witnesses he requires to put to the pursuer the points that he hopes will emerge from the evidence of Barnes etc. This is to give the pursuer a fair chance to respond. So he would have to put to the pursuer questions such as "We may hear evidence later from Mr Barnes that some of the timber planks were split, some were decayed and others showed unsightly staining whereas about a fifth had woodworm infestation. Would you dispute that this was the case?" You would then have a situation where the pursuer was having to comment on evidence which had not yet materialised, and might not even materialise in those terms. Having a witness respond to future hypothetical evidence is unsatisfactory. It is also very disadvantageous to the defender because there is a risk that the evidence of the defender or one of his witnesses will deviate from that version as put to the pursuer or that it will include matters not put to the pursuer at all. In addition, the defender is likely to want to listen to the cross examination of the pursuer (which, as a party, he is entitled to do) and will then be giving his evidence in the knowledge of the pursuer's position in relation to it.

If this all sounds convoluted and complicated it is supposed to, and it will have demonstrated why it is far better for the defender to lead and why it disadvantages the defender if he does not do so. The obvious solution is for the defender's agent to move the court to ordain the defender to lead; such a motion could not conceivably be opposed. No doubt the sheriff would be delighted to grant it. Doing so would make her task far easier than would be the case if the pursuer led.

At one time there would have been another issue, namely what is the mode of proof? This used to be an issue at Options Hearings in the mid 1990s.

CHAPTER 11

MODES OF PROOF

Prior to the Requirements of Writing (Scotland) Act 1995 some matters were capable of proof only by written evidence. For example, if I claimed to have been gifted £5000 by you in 1993 and you stated that the money was actually provided for safekeeping I would be constrained to proving the alleged gift by means of evidence in writing. This could be a letter or card from you acknowledging the gift, for example. My oral testimony would not be enough, even if I were to be believed by the court.

The rule was actually very sensible. It meant, that people were encouraged to take the precautions of getting written receipts and IOUs when they parted with money and wanted the opportunity to get it back. That way, there was certainty.

In some older textbooks you will find references to modes of proof. On allowing a proof the court would state the mode of that proof. There were three possibilities;

1) Written proof only.

2) Written, oral or real (known as proof *prout de jure*).

3) Proof *habili modo*. This meant that some disputed issues were provable by written evidence and some could be proved by any means.

It is arguable that pre-1995 actings are still provable under the pre-1995 law of evidence, even in an action raised now. O.C.R. 29.1 allows reference to oath despite that mechanism having been abolished by Section 11(1) of the 1995 Act, which provides that "Any rule of law and any enactment whereby the proof of any matter is restricted to proof by writ or by reference to oath shall cease to have effect." However, there is a saving provision in Section 14, which states that "nothing in this Act shall (a)apply to any document executed or anything done before the commencement of this Act. There is conflicting and non-binding case law on the interaction of Sections 11 and 14.

Despite the 1995 Act it is worth knowing about these rules because they can still be relevant. I conducted a case in 2008, which went to proof in 2011 and which concerned alleged loans made in 1994 and 1995 (all prior to the coming into effect of the 1995 Act) to a person who had died prior to the raising of the action. Although I was unsuccessful in persuading the court that the alleged loans were provable only by written evidence (of which there was none) the sheriff was influenced in his decision to assoilzie the defenders by the fact that at the time that the loans were alleged to have been made they were unprovable. In other words, had they been made it was surprising that the pursuer, as lender, would not have obtained written evidence.

The relevance of modes of proof has diminished as claims in respect of pre-1995 matters have become time-barred, but it is worth being aware of this area of law, if only to be able to understand some of the old law reports.

The position was even more complicated prior to the Prescription and Limitation (Scotland) Act 1973 when there was a range of prescriptive periods (including a "sexennium") after which time certain obligations could be proved only by written evidence.

CHAPTER 12

MANAGING THE EVIDENCE THAT YOU NEED TO SUCCEED AT A PROOF

Essentially, evidence takes three forms, real evidence, documentary productions and the testimony of witnesses (including affidavits). Technically there might be a fourth, locus inspection, although such visits are extremely rare. In an ideal world in which the best evidence was being used and cost was no obstacle there would be a locus inspection in every road traffic proof on liability. The sheriff would go and look at the junction where the accident happened.

(a) Real evidence means items other than documents that you show to the court. These are lodged in advance. Usually, you will find that the sheriff clerks hate real evidence, because they have to find space to store it. Also, some real evidence can be very valuable; I had a case in which a diamond ring was used. In another a fur jacket was lodged. This type of evidence is effective where you want to make a more forceful impression than would be created by a perusal of photographs. It is especially helpful in relation to logos or small tangible items where there is an importance in their finish and appearance, such as a restaurant menu, a liqueur bottle, a chair for use in a beer garden and a design on T-shirts, pens, car stickers and keyrings. I have used real evidence in all these examples, to good effect.

Photographs are a species of real evidence and often a very effective form. They are now standard in road traffic accident cases to show the scene of an accident and vehicle damage. Aerial photographs are ideal to show road layouts.

Video evidence can have great impact too. I have used this very effectively in anti-social conduct proofs. If you are going to use video evidence you need to ensure that you have worked out in advance how you are going to show it. The sheriff clerk used to be quite resistant to making equipment available You would be asked to bring your own equipment only to be told that it couldn't be used without being tested for health and safety purposes. To be fair, this is far less of a problem than it used to be, although you should always flag these issues up with the sheriff clerk weeks or months in advance.

The same comments applies with audio evidence. I recall a Child Welfare Hearing in which an agent played a recording of a father trying to cause trouble during a telephone conversation with the child. Such material can be a very effective form of evidence. Note Chapter 50 of the Ordinary Cause Rules, which makes special provisions for lodging audio and audio-visual recordings of children.

Text messages you would print out and lodge as documentary productions.

(b) Documentary Productions; I have seen numerous problems arise in relation to these.

First and foremost, do not lodge anything that you do not understand. Technical language can be checked on the internet. You have to acquire a working knowledge of the areas under scrutiny in the action, regardless of how obscure they are. Court lawyers find themselves experts, albeit temporarily, in all manner of weird and wonderful topics.

There is a skill in deciding how much to lodge insofar as having enough to prove your case whilst keeping detrimental material out without making it conspicuous by its absence. If you lodge a forty-page bank statement that is missing page 22, your opponent (and the court) is bound to want to know what is on that missing page. If there is something on page 22 that you do not want disclosed, try to achieve that by omitting other pages too, the more the better, or use samples.

Generally, there is a temptation to lodge absolutely everything available. This is comparable to pleading everything that you might need to rely upon, or including in your witness list everyone you can possibly think of; and it is to do with being safe rather than sorry. You do not need to use a production that you have lodged but (subject to the sheriff's discretion) you are not allowed to use one that you have not lodged.

Try not to succumb to this temptation. If you do lodge everything do not make it look obvious that you have, because you do not want your opponent to know that you have no other cards to play, as it were.

Do not lodge documents that you plan to produce to an unsuspecting witness during cross-examination. These need to be kept in reserve and undisclosed.

Bear in mind too that volume of productions is a factor in whether an uplift in expenses should be granted. So if you lodge many hundreds of items and your client loses the case, that deluge of productions may justify a motion by the opponent to have his expenses inflated by a percentage uplift (Rule 5.2(6)(c) of the 2019 Rules). On the other hand, if you win but most of your own productions were unnecessary that would not be a good basis for an uplift of your own expenses.

Productions have to be user friendly to the sheriff and to any witness who is speaking to them. Also, if your witness is remote, you need to get copy productions to him in plenty of time for the proof. You can have the witness look at documents on the screen, but in my view that is risky- the witness might have technical issues or be uncomfortable using technology, and you can easily waste time.

Presentation of documentary evidence ought to follow a system. If you have a set of invoices, delivery notes and receipts relating to a building claim either lodge them chronologically, or by the names of the supplier or by the type of document; all the invoices together, followed by all delivery notes then all receipts. There is no requirement under the rules to do this. You may list productions in an inventory in any order you like, or in no order whatsoever. In an emergency, where you are lodging a writ and inventory in a hurry in order to get an interim inhibition or interdict, neatness may have to be sacrificed a little.

Check that the productions are in process, that they are numbered, that they are in order and there is a copy for the sheriff. This sounds obvious but never assume that all is in order. In my experience these kinds of issues raise problems in a lot of proofs. It irritates the sheriff, wastes time, interrupts business and makes you look amateurish. Tab your own copy so that you are not fumbling about trying to find them.

If you have a production that is a dozen pages long, unnumbered, number the pages so that if you want to refer a witness or the court to a particular page or passage you do not have the witness flapping about in the witness box trying to find that page or passage. Remember that a witness box is not a lectern and is rarely designed to let the witness organise papers easily. They often have no surface on which to lean anything other than the edge of the witness box, which can be 4 inches from top to bottom.

Remember that productions are either probative (self-proving) or not. A land certificate is probative whereas an unwitnessed letter is not. If a production is not probative it needs a witness to speak to it unless it is admitted or agreed.

Consider what you are setting out to prove and how you are trying to use the production to prove it. Take a breach of missives case where you act for the buyer, who discovered that the central heating system was a disaster and had to get a new boiler and associated plumbing fitted. Depending on whether the work has been done you would probably lodge an invoice or estimate from a plumber. If it is an invoice your client can certainly say in evidence "I received and paid this invoice". That is good evidence of those facts. But if the defence is that the sum sued for is excessive, that evidence is not enough to prove that the sum sued for is not excessive. You would need the evidence of the plumber (or another plumber) to speak to that.

Sheriffs will sometimes get impatient because you do not agree evidence. Whether there is legitimate impatience depends on whether it is reasonable and sensible that you do so.

For example, consider the *ex facie* provenance of a production. A statement of an account held with a well-known High Street bank is pretty unlikely to be a fake. One would be expected to agree that. On the other hand, an invoice from a sole trader who happens to be your client's opponent's cousin does not carry the same weight. One would not be expected to agree that.

Some sheriffs will try to pressurise you into agreeing productions. But remember that agreeing evidence is something that you can do only on your client's instructions. Never do this off your own bat. Bear in mind the obvious that if your opponent asks you to agree evidence it is because it is advantageous to him and almost certainly correspondingly disadvantageous to your client. So why make your opponent's job easier?

Making Concessions

Sheriffs will sometimes put you under pressure to make concessions. For example, that there was not compelling enough evidence to support a finding in fact that you were asking the court to make. Be extremely careful about conceding anything. From a self-preservation perspective it is far better to have a judge repel your submission rather than not to make it at all. As *Macphail* says at 16.102 "concessions should be made with care".

Some sheriffs intervene far too much in asking questions during a proof. Traditionally they are supposed to keep out of it unless there is some point that needs to be clarified. In practice I have seen cases where the sheriff is asking more questions than the agent. This can be a problem, because you cannot very well object to a question from the bench. It is irritating to have to hear a sheriff put a question that your opponent had forgotten to ask or which would have been met with objection had he remembered to put it.

More helpfully, during the course of a proof a sheriff may look at you with a knowing or baffled or slightly pained look. If so, take note. Such signals can be important. They will never appear in the shorthand notes or in an audio recording of the evidence but they can often be a cue for you to object or to react later in cross-examination.

If you do not agree a matter of evidence or fact and the opponent forgets to lead proof of it (for example by overlooking the need to ask a witness a couple of questions about it) your client might avoid liability to pay part of the sum sued for. Taking advantage of such a blunder may seem unfair, but remember that litigation is adversarial.

The reasons for agreeing evidence may be several. Firstly, reciprocity; you might find that if you agree some of your opponent's productions he will agree some of yours. Secondly, there might be productions that could undoubtedly be proved if your opponent were forced to go to the trouble of calling a witness to speak to them. So, to take the bank statement example, it's pointless to dispute an *ex facie* authentic bank statement because otherwise, your opponent will simply call an official from the bank to speak to it. And although your opponent would have to pay that witness' expenses in the first instance, it is almost certain that your client would be paying them in terms of an award of expenses made by the sheriff. And my view is that your client would be penalised in those expenses even if he won the case. Bear in mind that a successful party can be found liable in expenses of part of the procedure or of the whole case, if he has been unreasonable (*Macphail* 19.15)

Requiring a bank official to attend would be regarded as unreasonable unless you had a legitimate reason to doubt the authenticity or accuracy of the production. And this is a situation where the sheriff would be entitled to be annoyed.

Note that in actions proceeding to proof in relation to Section 11 orders relating to children (e.g. contact) there is a chapter, No. 33AA, in the O.C.R.s headed "Expeditious Resolution of Certain Causes". The sheriff can restrict issues for proof and exclude specific documents, reports and witnesses from proof. That level of shrieval control is the way that all litigation is going, in my view.

(c) Witnesses

The 2020 Act provides generally for dispensing with physical attendance and with attendance by remote means, but there has been a huge volume of Guidance Notes issued by the sheriffs principal, and you have to be mindful of these. For example, an unnumbered Guidance on Management of Civil Business in the Sheriffdom of Grampian, Highland and Islands from 2020 provided that parties are responsible for ensuring that any witnesses do not arrive earlier than 10 minutes before a time to be agreed with the court. These are the kinds of logistical management issues of which you have to be aware.

Identifying potential witnesses

You should be looking to recover evidence as soon as you are instructed in a case. As regards witness evidence, sometimes it can become apparent at a very early point that someone is likely to be called to attend court to give evidence. If someone is at death's door or about to emigrate to Australia you need to obtain an affidavit to capture and preserve that evidence.

Those who become witnesses sometimes struggle to appreciate that they have acquired this new status. Once somebody acquires the status of being a potential witness she must be treated with caution. So you may find that a client's mother accompanies her to your office to provide moral support. That is fine, but if you decide that she should be called as a witness, perhaps to corroborate your client's account, you need to be careful that as a source of evidence she remains as impartial and independent as possible. Also, you do not want her to be sitting in your office along with the client being influenced by advice or information given by you to the client or by information given by the client to you.

Having accurate precognitions is essential. These should as far as possible be a prediction of that which the precognosee is likely to say in response to being questioned in a witness box. Some precognitions will include statements such as "An interdict is necessary to prevent conduct injurious to my wellbeing." For a start, no lay person would say this. Secondly, it parrots a legal opinion that the person is not qualified to make. Only expert witnesses are entitled to offer opinion evidence. Lastly, it affords no help whatsoever to the solicitor who may end up examining this person as a witness. Stick to facts, explained in the language that the precognosee actually uses, and include the basis on which the person is qualified to give that information, such as "I saw him hit her" rather than "he hit her".

Omitting unfavourable facts does no-one any favours. It was stated in *Kerr v HMA* SLT 82 that "Pregognosers as a whole appear to be gifted with a measure of optimism which no amount of disillusionment appears to damp".

If you decide to call the precognosee as a witness (and you may decide not to do so, of course) make sure that he knows why. Do not coach the witness or tell him what you want him to say, identify the material that he has given in his precognition and that this is why he is being called to give evidence.

Some solicitors get precognosees to sign their precognitions. This is a good idea. Or you can send it to them. If it is a really significant statement, e.g. that a solicitor has committed a fraud, it is prudent to obtain an affidavit, i.e. a statement given under oath. Or get a colleague to take a precognition separately and outwith your presence. This is important for self-protection.

Macphail 15.10 says that you should always precognose one witness outwith the presence of another. This is crucial. Again, it mirrors the fact that witnesses give evidence individually and separately, and without a friend or relative or colleague sitting beside the witness box interjecting.

After you have cited them or told them to attend court, phone witnesses and remind them that they are attending court and reiterate to them the town in which the court is situated. It is not uncommon for someone to go to the sheriff court in Paisley instead of Glasgow or to Hamilton instead of Airdrie. Tell witnesses about parking, the nearest train station etc. Get their mobile numbers and write it down on your file.

Warn them that they may have a long wait, that they might want to bring a book, and that they should meet you somewhere specific; eg inside the front door of the court at a particular time, half an hour before the proof is due to start.

Witnesses sometimes ask about dress code. Tell them to look smart. That shows respect to the court. This does not need to be a suit and tie, but avoid e.g. a white tracksuit and definitely avoid football strips even if your client is really a centre-half with Rangers. Before they make arrangements to attend a West of Scotland court, tell your client not to wear green or blue or orange. Avoid chewing gum.

Explain to your witnesses what they have to do; i.e. go into the witness box, take an oath and answer questions. It might seem obvious to you, but it will not be to most people. Tell them that you are not allowed to ask questions which indicate the answer you want and that they should, if possible, give expansive answers, unprompted, which enable evidence to be put before the court. Make eye contact with the sheriff and try not to speak too quickly.

If witnesses are going to speak to documents let them see them before they enter the witness box rather than once they are there.

Witnesses derive a lot of their expectations from television and films, much of it American. They think that there will be a jury, that they will have to swear on a bible and say "So help me God" at the end of their oath.

Tell your client and witnesses not to use your first name; that never looks good. And tell them to switch their mobile phones off.

Tell them also to avoid posting anything about the case on social media. This can be especially unwise before cross examination, during which posted comments can be cast up with embarrassing results.

In my experience a witness undoubtedly possesses an advantage if he is articulate, well presented and polite. This is unfair, because such an individual is no more inherently credible or reliable for having these attributes. In addition, some witnesses are more accustomed than others in dealing on a daily basis with professional people. They too will generally fare better in a formal environment such as a courtroom. So what to do if your client lacks these advantages? The best way of enabling them to give their evidence in the most beneficial way is to make them feel as much as possible at ease and to demystify the process. It is surprising how many witnesses do not know what to expect

Good communication is key. Clients will be far more comfortable in a courtroom if they have developed trust, familiarity and rapport with the lawyer who is there to represent them. This is one of the areas where the agency solicitor is at a disadvantage.

Once witnesses have all turned up at the court they are supposed to be enclosed in the witness room, responsibility for which, as with so many other responsibilities, falls to the solicitor.

Witnesses should be advised by the solicitors citing them not to discuss a case while waiting to give evidence and shouldn't disclose the evidence they've given to witnesses yet to give their evidence. They should be discouraged from mixing with witnesses yet to give evidence.

Quarantining witnesses is not always easy or even possible. Some proof courts simply do not possess witness rooms; e.g. Court 9 in Glasgow. People are often hanging about at court. Often, they are related, or they are friends or work colleagues. And, being nervous strangers in a strange land they seek comfort in chatting to those they know. If you have a divorce client who has travelled there with a friend or relative it is inconceivable that they will not succumb to the temptation to discuss the case.

However, you have to try to stop that, and you have to be seen to be trying to stop it. So, tell your client or witness in the presence of your opposite number and the bar officer and the sheriff clerk "Do not discuss your evidence with anyone". The sheriff may say that to him too, which is helpful.

A problem can arise where a proof is adjourned to another day, especially whilst somebody is in the middle of giving evidence. If it is adjourned for a month and your client isn't finished his evidence, may you meet with him in between times? *Greens Annotated Rules of the Court of Session* states at 36.9.1 that "Counsel and agents may not discuss with a witness during an adjournment the evidence he is giving."

So, yes, you can have a meeting, but ask yourself whether it is wise to do that. It probably is not.

CHAPTER 13

INTIMATING AND LODGING LISTS OF DOCUMENTS, WITNESSES, AFFIDAVITS AND PRODUCTIONS

The Covid rules have had a major impact on how this is done; broadly speaking, the sheriff clerk does not want you sending hard copies of anything. You need to check the procedure in the court where you are litigating, and to do it in plenty of time.

In practice, many solicitors ignore the standard rules about deadlines, and so do many sheriffs as long as there is no material prejudice. But, such slackness is dangerous as well as being needless. You cannot assume that you will be able to escape the consequences of disregarding the rules. Somebody might be dogmatic; a party litigant, an awkward colleague, an over-zealous sheriff. To be fair, you cannot criticise somebody too much for objecting; after all, it is in your client's opponent's interests to object to your late productions or list of witnesses. He will not care a whit (nor should he) if you get into bother.

If something is late then you can ask the court to use its dispensing power to allow it in late. And as long as your opponent will not be unfairly prejudiced, you will probably succeed. But never assume anything. Remember that the consequences of a late list can be disastrous. We all tend to be too blasé about this. And if you had evidence with instructions to lodge it in time and you did not do so that is negligence, and you are leaving yourself exposed to a claim or a complaint.

In practice, rather than forcing you to run a proof without important evidence a court would probably discharge the proof. There will then arise the awkward issue of the expenses of that. The tab will have to be picked up either by your client (who will blame you) or you; you can be found personally liable. Either way, you will end up paying, and you will look daft.

So you need to check the rules to make sure you do not fall foul of them. And do not assume that they are all the same; they are not. In some the reference date for a time limit is that of the order allowing the proof and in others it is that of the proof itself.

In Ordinary Causes, you must intimate to your opponent within 14 days of the interlocutor allowing a proof a list of the documents that you are going to use at the proof. These "documents" are not synonymous with productions. Documents in this context comprise written material that you have not yet lodged as productions, and might technically never do so. For that reason you do not lodge anything under this rule, you merely intimate a list; O.C.R .9A.2.

In addition, you have 28 days from the interlocutor allowing proof to intimate and lodge a list of witnesses; O.C.R. 9A.3. Although caution may suggest that you name Uncle Tom Cobley and all, remember that the opponent may well speak to everyone on the list, incurring an expense that your client might end up bearing, Also, at least one of those listed might say something adverse, to your opponent's advantage.

In Ordinary Causes you have to get your Productions lodged at least 28 days before the proof; OCR 29.11.

Watch too that there are special rules for personal injury cases. There is an O.C.R. 36.G1 ("Allocation of diets and timetables") which refers to Appendix 3 to the O.C.R.s. The Sheriff Principal may vary these time limits, and would do that by Practice Note.

The level of micro-management in personal injury cases is extreme, as it is in so many areas of litigation including procedure before the Sheriff Appeal Court. That is the shape of things to come generally, in my view.

CHAPTER 14

PRACTICAL STEPS TO MAKE LIFE AS EASY AS POSSIBLE ON THE DAY

It is said that a proof concentrates the mind wonderfully, and this is true. Imagine, six weeks before the proof itself that you are having to start at 10am the following morning. Write out a list of questions or points. Whatever you do have a structure of some kind. For one thing, a script is a safety net whilst you walk the tightrope; if you get distracted, or you panic, or lose your train of thought, you have a script to go back to. In addition, in my opinion writing out questions in advance is the best way of preparing for a proof. You familiarise yourself with the material that you intend to use (although you should never forget to get well acquainted with the opponent's productions too), you work out when you require to refer to productions, for example; and you can number the production in your list of questions, in a different colour of pen.

But don't be tied to the script; a list of questions can be restrictive and inflexible. Even if you do a flow chart of questions; if the witness answers "yes" you go down one route and if "no" you follow another. You have to be able to think on your feet. Proofs rarely always go to plan. They often take on a life of their own, sometimes turbulently, and take twists and turns which were not foreseeable. You can easily find yourself wending your way along unfamiliar highways and byways when, for example, a witness says something completely at odds with the contents of his precognition.

Remember too that your opponent might get away with lodging a late production or calling an extra witness or will start exploring a line of evidence of which you had had no real notice. Also, it is permitted to ambush a witness with a prior inconsistent statement, never lodged as a production, with a view to challenging either credibility or reliability. Never assume that the opponent's productions exhaust the material that he possesses; he may have something explosive up his sleeve.

You could just mirror the pleadings rather than drawing up a list of questions, but often that is inadequate; the pleadings are too brief, they rarely refer to all the productions and you may well need to get a witness to develop a point.

The courtroom environment

The layout of a proof court varies enormously. There is a lot of luck involved. Some are very badly designed. In my experience the table is usually too low, leading to bad posture, back strain and a difficulty in writing. A pursuer and his agent should sit to the right of the sheriff (looking from the back of the court) and if the witness box is also on the right the agent may require Houdini-like contortionist abilities to face the witness and sheriff whilst being able to access papers and copy productions and to write down notes. Multi-tasking is an essentially ability in conducting a proof single-handedly. If possible, have a colleague there to take notes. Counsel has a far easier job than a solicitor in that there is an instructing agent present to record the evidence whilst the advocate focusses on the questioning.

The question of having a client sit right beside you during a proof is a matter of discretion. It can be a distraction. On the other hand, you need to be accessible. Clients can feel isolated and detached from the proceedings if they cannot speak to you and, after all, it is their case, not yours. Clients will sometimes ask you to put a question to a witness. This can be a tricky situation because it can happen when you are under stress and without a lot of time to think and to react. This can be a problem. You have to follow instructions, but at the same time it might be a stupid instruction. My view is that you should try to talk the client out of it (get an adjournment to discuss, if necessary). I had a divorce proof in Kilmarnock where the client, who was sitting beside me said to me during my cross examination of her husband "Ask him if he withdrew cash from his bank account and spent it on a motorbike" This frivolous expenditure had never been mentioned by anyone before and there was no way of proving that he'd spend money on a motorbike or not. If he denies it, I whispered to her, won't he just deny it? No, she said, he won't. My view at the time was that it was foolish to ask that question, because it if he denied spending money on a motorbike it would look worse than if he hadn't been asked at all. What I should have done was to have asked for a 5-minute adjournment and explained this to the client. But I didn't. I was reluctant to ask the question but, more importantly, I didn't want her to complain if I didn't ask it. So I asked if he'd bought a motorbike. "No" came the response. And that was that.

If you focus on keeping yourself right (ie asking that question) you will usually be serving the client's interest too. But there are exceptions, and that is one. Clients do not always know what is best for them. On that point, here's another scenario, also in Kilmarnock.

I was defending a breach of missives case on quantum only. The issue was whether my client had seen that the buyer's daughter was in a wheelchair when the family was viewing the house. In my opinion the Pursuer's evidence didn't show that it was likely that he had seen it. He hadn't been at the viewing, but had driven past in his car. My feeling, which I conveyed to him, was that on balance he should not give evidence. But he was adamant that he wanted to. And, during cross examination he conceded that he possibly had spotted the wheelchair. And he lost the proof.

On a similar point to that of the distracting client, you might choose to keep your client out of the courtroom whilst others are giving evidence. I have persuaded a client not to be present where I considered that he was likely to be intimidating to a witness. Or, the client might be unable to stop tutting, sighing, rolling his eyes or fidgeting annoyingly.

Your client needs to agree to leave, of course, because he is entitled to be there and it is understandable why he would want to be; something might crop up on which you want to take instructions. Also, it can look as if the client lacks interest if he is not there, so give the sheriff a reason why he is sitting outside; for example in case the opponent might feel uncomfortable.

Clients sometimes think that unless they are in the witness box they are somehow shielded from scrutiny by the sheriff. This is a delusion. Unfortunately, in my experience some sheriffs expect clients to retain a Zen-like state of serenity in the midst of one of the most stressful environments possible, where the fate of their family, business or solvency may be at stake and where they encounter hostility and possess a feeling of impotence. It is understandable that clients become offended, frustrated and angry while a witness is traducing them or even giving an account which differs from theirs. Courtrooms are stressful places. Nobody really wants to be there. Whilst this unpleasantness is not intentional it is also true that litigation is meant to be a last resort and that proceeding to a proof is the final step of that resort. Sheriffs would much rather that parties settled instead.

Familiarise yourself with the courtroom if you can; this is more difficult now that the wholesale removal of procedural civil business means that the proof may be the only time that your case ever calls. I conducted a hearing in front of a licensing board a few years ago. I had never been in that venue before and I was not prepared for the format. I had not realised how numerous the councillors would be, how high up they would be sitting (higher than on any bench I have seen in any sheriff court) and how so many of those appearing -my client amongst them – would be so relentlessly bombarded with hostile questions. If I had visited to observe this board in action a week or so before I would have been more comfortable when I appeared myself.

Be careful what you say in front of the sheriff clerk or bar officer. Never say anything that you would not want the sheriff to know. Because things can get communicated.

Getting rid of distractions

This can often be a problem in family cases. You arrived at court, stressed and trying to focus on the task and you get distracted by friends or relatives of the client asking questions; and you just want them to go away. In those circumstances, where it is the client's own interests that you are able to concentrate on the job at hand, consider telling the distractor that you might need to use him as a witness; which means that, alas, he cannot be there when you are discussing matters with your client. This is a tactic that you can use in the office or at court. Of course, you do not need to have cited somebody to call him as a witness.

Coloured pens

These should be as prevalent in proofs as in nursery school. I remember being in a proof where I had counsel and the opponent had a Q.C. who later became an Inner House judge. He had with him a whole pencil case full of coloured pencils. Everyone conducting a proof should deploy coloured pens or pencils or highlighters When you are in flow during a proof you will have a list of questions or points. If those are in black ink use a red pen to write down the witness' answers. There is nothing worse that scribbling down questions, desired answers and actual answers and getting them mixed up after the proof has finished.

Or, even more excruciating; you put it to a witness during cross examination that he said something during his evidence in chief, and it turns out that he did nothing of the sort; your monochrome notes are wrong. You will look stupid in front of the witness, undermining your authority.

Taking notes is vitally important. It can be difficult too; particularly if you are questioning a witness at the same time and especially during cross examination. I conducted a Court of Session proof several years ago where I had someone with me taking notes on some days but where I was on my own on other days, and the difference in pressure was enormous.

Fraternising with the enemy

Lawyers feel the stress of the courtroom. They also often know each other. It is easy, frequently too easy, to ease and calm the tension by a joke or friendly word to the solicitor on the other side. This is an area where great care is required. Clients may not appreciate their agent (for whose attendance they are paying handsomely) having a giggle with the lawyer who, as they see it, is the enemy. They may question your loyalty. They may wonder whose side you truly represent. They may see a conspiracy. We all know that it is often a question of chance or providence that we act for one party rather than another, and we are taught and trained that it is nothing personal and that we are all simply doing a job. Clients do not have that outlook, however. For them, it is personal. This is not to advocate coldness towards colleagues. Far from it. It is merely to suggest that it is better to save the banter and mirth for when the clients are no longer present.

Fraternising with the client

Be friendly towards but do not befriend your clients. This merely results in their feeling more the bitter sting of disappointment in the event of the case not going their way because they will feel let down by you more personally.

Clients often make fickle friends. Be careful about telling the client anything unflattering about the sheriff or the agents. If that client complains he will have the power to tell the SLCC that you said that the sheriff is an idiot. Client confidentiality does not cut both ways; it is designed to protect the client, not the lawyer. In other words, you are precluded from telling the world at large that your client wanted you to present a fraudulent document in court, but the client is quite at liberty to tell everyone that you were willing to do so (assuming that you were so crooked, unscrupulous and unethical as to do so).

Napoleon Bonaparte is said to have remarked, very shrewdly, that one should never interrupt one's enemy when he is making a mistake. Do not draw your opponent's attention to something significant that someone has said, especially something damaging that his client has said in evidence. In numerous cases I have observed my opponent writing something down and underlining it, or even adding exclamation marks. Often you do not require the skill of being able to read upside down to know what has prompted this exuberant outburst. This unwitting disclosure is more likely to happen in those courtrooms where there is a couple of metres between you and the other agents.

You have to be poker faced; if something emerges out that is damaging to your client's case try to avoid looking horrified or dismayed (even if you feel that way to the very core of your being). Similarly, try not to look delighted if unexpectedly favourable evidence comes out.

Only a scoundrel could condone tactics such as causing your opponent discomfort by highlighting or underline your notes visibly and randomly. Neither could one approve of the solicitor in Glasgow (later a sheriff) who would bring books to proofs simply to rattle his opponents. *Prescription and Limitation* by David Johnston was a favourite, sowing unsettling doubts that the proof would conclude with a blindsiding argument of time bar.

Never draw a weakness or an omission to your opponent's attention until it is too late for him to do anything about it.

Here is an example; I had a divorce proof where the husband opponent claimed that he could not work due to back problems. He did not aver in his pleadings nor say in evidence that he had seen a doctor. He had lodged no medical evidence. During cross examination I could have pointed this out and asked him if he had ever done anything about his allegedly malfunctioning back. But that would simply have alerted him to the problem and he could then have lied and said that he had been to see his doctor. And I could not have contradicted him. To deprive him of that opportunity to rectify a flaw in his case, I simply stated in submissions after the proof had closed that there was no evidence that the husband had ever seen a doctor; and the sheriff made the appropriate finding in fact.

CHAPTER 15

USING EVIDENCE AT THE PROOF; WITNESSES

Pace of questioning

When you are questioning witnesses try to go slowly. Most solicitors go too quickly, without realising it. There are different reasons for this. If you are nervous there is a tendency to gallop. If you have written down your questions you may assume that everyone in the courtroom as is familiar with them as you are, and it can seem reasonable to speed through them. If you are trying to pin down a witness who is being evasive or slippery there can be the temptation to batter him with a barrage of questions quickly so as to catch him out and prevent him having the time to make something up. You may encounter the opponent's witness who seems to develop deafness between examination in chief and cross examination; following an awkward question you will meet a pained expression and "Can you repeat the question please?" as he sneakily buys himself precious time to concoct an answer. It can be frustrating. And when you are cross examining an opportunist it may actually help your client's case to proceed swiftly. But remember that the sheriff is supposed to be writing down or typing notes of that which is said. If you go too fast the court might lose the place, interrupt and (worst still) might order the extension of the shorthand notes; we have seen how expensive that can be.

Leading questions;

Leading questions are structured in such a way as to suggest the answer which the questioner wants, These are generally forbidden, although a witness' personal details can be obtained this way, and leading questions can be asked on other matters not in dispute.

So, if it is agreed that a collision occurred between the parties vehicles on 1st January 2021 you should lead on that. Asking "when did the collision occur" is pointless and a waste of time. I would say to the witness "It is not in dispute that your car and that of Mr Duguid collided on 1st January 2023." And I would then go on to ask a question such as "Where were you driving immediately before that happened?" setting the scene so that the court can follow the account more easily.

Make questions intelligible.

When you are examining witnesses make sure that you ask a question that the witness is able to answer. For example, if you are asking about distances, ensure beforehand – during the precognition stage –_that the witness understands units of measurements. In my experience many people are hopeless at judging speed or distance, so asking "How many car lengths were you from the junction before you saw the other car?" will be answered with baffled guesswork. Such evidence is uselessly unreliable. Also, in road traffic cases we use imperial units when everywhere else is metric. How many drivers know the distance between a moving vehicle and a set of traffic lights at any given point? You could ask a question and get the answer, 10 car lengths, 100 feet, 100 metres etc. It is risky.

Depending on how the evidence comes out you can find yourself desperately trying to calculate the time it takes a car travelling at 30mph to collide with another vehicle doing 5mph in in the opposite direction 15 metres way. And the evidence is often unreliable anyway.

A precognition in which the witness has given a clear answer is reassuring, but the evidence might deviate wildly from the precognition.

I conducted a case of tripping in a street in Glasgow where at the end of the proof the sheriff remarked that in the course of that hour she had heard evidence about three different accidents. It was painfully clear from the outset that the Pursuer did not know his centimetres from his inches. The pavement had been repaired by the time of the proof and nobody had taken a photograph with a ruler or coin beside the tripping hazard (which is an excellent method of showing distance).

The best plan, in my view, in road traffic cases, is to show witnesses photographs.

Use language that the witness understands. So whilst you and the sheriff might know the meaning of locus, starboard or offside rear, a witness might very well be confused.

In my experience witnesses often tell you what they think must have happened rather than what they actually saw happen, especially if they are a passenger in a vehicle involved in a collision. They will say that they saw the other car change lanes suddenly and strike the offside rear, whereas sometimes you suspect that they have been focussed on Facebook and the first they know of the collision is when they feel a jolt and hear a bang.

CHAPTER 16

ADDUCING OBJECTIVE AND NOT SUBJECTIVE EVIDENCE

It is easy for witnesses to give subjective evidence. For instance a witness may state that her husband is a "heavy drinker, frequently intoxicated and regularly violent".

However, such evidence is useless, as being opinion evidence from someone who is there not to opine but to provide the court with the factual evidence that it needs so that it can reach an opinion.

As to whether someone is a heavy drinker you need evidence of what he drinks, the volume that he drinks and how often he does so. "frequently intoxicated" should be specified as most days, every week, each Friday night and so on and the witness should describes manifestations of intoxication that she has observed, such as shouting and swearing, slurred speech, falling down, walking into furniture, involuntary urination, the heavy odour of alcohol on breath and so on. You need specific evidence of the frequency and level of somebody's drinking before you can ask the sheriff to find in fact that it was heavy.

I had a neighbour nuisance case in which the client said in evidence that she was "frequently" disturbed by noise. You cannot leave it at that; you need evidence of facts; so you need to ask "In the last year how many times were you disturbed?" "Was there a disturbance every month?" Every week? How many days in the average week? At what times? For how long each time? Could you hear the noise when your TV was on at normal volume? It needs to be specific so that the sheriff can make an assessment of whether, to the reasonable person, the disturbance was frequent and that it was unreasonable and excessive.

Solatium is a tricky area, and asking a witness to describe pain calls for some care. It is the only evidence there will be. My technique is to ask how the witness felt immediately after the accident, an hour later, 24 hours later, a week, two weeks and so on. Use metaphors to describe the kind of pain, such as stabbing and burning, as well as more literal descriptions such as throbbing and aching. Ask how it altered over time, in intensity and duration and how it affected sleep, concentration, mood and other factors that the witness needs to describe personally.

Do not ask witnesses questions of law, such as "You owe the money, don't you?" You can ask if he has paid the money because that is a question of fact alone.

CHAPTER 17

CALLING WITNESSES

You choose the order in which witnesses are called. You would nearly always call your own client first. Firstly, he is usually the most important witness and you want to get that evidence out at the start and make an impression when the sheriff is fresh and paying the most attention. Secondly, the client is almost certainly going to want to sit in court with you after having given evidence, so you want to make sure that he gives his evidence before hearing other people's evidence. Then you'd possibly have a witness to corroborate what he has said, or to provide information beyond what your client has said. If you have an expert witness or somebody giving evidence of a technical nature you would probably call him towards the end, when the scene has been set for their involvement by the evidence given by the other witnesses.

There is research to show that the court's attention peaks at the start and at the end of a proof, with a trough in the centre. Some might observe that in this sense it is akin to a stage play. Anyway, the trough is the place to bury bad news; detrimental but unavoidable features of your own case should be raised in this mid-point.

On a related topic, you should try to dampen your opponent's squib. Every case has its weaknesses. Generally, it lessens their impact if they are raised and explored (and diminished, if possible) by you pre-emptively, rather than being first mentioned by your opponent.

Be careful if you are defending a case on behalf of a non-natural person (eg a limited company) If you want to lead the evidence of the director who is instructing you on behalf of the company you need to bear in mind that because the director is separate from the Defender company he is not a party and therefore he is not entitled to be present or hear the evidence of other witnesses before he gives his own evidence. Check with your opponent weeks ahead of the proof whether there will be an objection. And if there is not make sure that you also obtain the sheriff's agreement in advance.

In the lap of the Gods

Once a proof starts you have lost control. This be a shock, especially for agents who settle 90% of their cases and suddenly find themselves in an environment where they cannot stop a witness from saying the wrong thing.

Neither do you know until it has started how well somebody performs in the witness box. People can react unpredictably under pressure. The exuberant orator sitting in your office can become a sullen introvert in the witness box. Less often, the reverse might occur. Another phenomenon is that a witness who is dull and reticent during examination in chief then feels under attack and becomes assertive under cross examination, giving the very evidence that the examiner in chief had been seeking in vain.

Do not ask unnecessary questions; if something is admitted in the pleadings do not waste time or take risks asking witnesses about it. For example if you are acting for a father in a family case never ask him the date of birth of his child. If he gets it right it adds nothing to the evidence (because the date will be on a birth certificate, which is a probative document) and if he gets it wrong he looks stupid. The more evidence you bring out the greater the scope for something going wrong. So bring out the evidence that you need, but go easy otherwise.

CHAPTER 18

CREDIBILITY VERSUS RELIABILITY

There is an important distinction. The former but not the latter concerns honesty. If a witness is incredible he or she is a liar. If the witness is unreliable he or she is honest but mistaken. Somebody might be both.

If you can get away with submitting that a witness is unreliable (rather than incredible) do that. Unreliable evidence is as weak as incredible evidence and people generally are more likely to be mistaken than dishonest. So try to rely on unreliability, especially if the witness is an official such as a police officer, or has no apparent axe to grind. For example a passer-by who sees a road traffic accident has no obvious reason to lie under oath.

However, if there is no scope for error you have to put it to a witness that he is not being truthful. This can feel awkward. I had a case in which my client claimed that the opponent's alleged passenger had not been in the car at all. I had to put that to him. In another case the client claimed that a solicitor had doctored her file to include a faked file note of a conversation that he said had never happened. There was no possibility of mistake, so I had to put to her the extraordinarily serious charge that she had made up the conversation and had inserted this fictitious file note.

It is sometimes said that solicitors lose debates, clients lose proofs. What that means is that if your client is found to be unreliable or incredible that is not your fault. But that is not necessarily correct.

Assume that the issue is whether your client reported something by email. He says in evidence that he gave his lawyer (you) the email. Assume that he has, but that you have not lodged it. The sheriff will assume, and will be entitled to assume, either than he is lying when he says that he gave you the email or that it does not say what he says it says. This is because the court will expect that if you possess such evidence you would have lodged it. So if you have not lodged it is because you do not possess it.

So you can see here that if you blunder, the consequence could be that your client is disbelieved, or found to be unreliable when he should not be.

The best kind of incredibility (from the perspective of the agent) is where the sheriff just has the gut feeling that the witness is at it. It can be hard for a sheriff to articulate this instinctive impression in a judgment. Usually it will say that the witness was evasive or belligerent; which is not quite the same as saying that he seemed like a rogue or a rascal. Appeal courts almost never interfere with the assessment of reliability or credibility by a court of first instance, of course.

CHAPTER 19

OBJECTING TO THE OPPONENT'S QUESTIONS

Two points;

1) Do it quickly. If you dilly dally and the witness starts answering you might be taken to have waived your right to object. You need to be concentrating on what is happening all the time and ready to take action if you need to. It can take only seconds for irreparable damage to be inflicted upon your client's case. You need to be listening carefully to see where things are going, and to be able to spring to your feet with the agility of a gazelle; this is one of the reasons why running a proof can be stressful.

2) You are objecting to the answer, not the question. The latter is not evidence of anything. The answer is. So if witness is asked an innocuous question but starts answering it by giving an account that is absent from the Record or was not put to your client or is irrelevant you have to object as soon as that starts to happen. If a question necessarily invites an objectionable answer leap up nimbly and object to the question before the witness starts answering it.

CHAPTER 20

CROSS EXAMINATION

Some lawyers approach this with the belief that they can break the will and spirit of a witness with ruthless and aggressive questioning. This approach is often counterproductive. It frequently looks like bullying, putting the sheriff uncomfortably on guard as to whether he should step in. Also, people usually become defensive, and will try to justify what they have said already by re-enforcing it. Voices can be raised, tempers fray, questions levelled in both directions; all very undignified.

A great deal of cross examination is far too belligerent. Remember that you are not there to rebuke someone For one thing, remember that the opponent's account of event may be completely truthful and accurate.

Witnesses expect a hard time during cross examination. They worry too that deviating from evidence already given by them will land them in bother. It sometimes yields rewards to be nice to them, their relief manifesting itself in a greater willingness to admit the possibility of error in their account of events.

Another tactic can be to pause after the witness has answered, implying that there is more that one had expected to hear, to the discomfiture of the witness.

Some witnesses who are put under intense cross-examination will react by speaking with far more candour and feeling than they displayed under examination in chief. This creates risk. It could be that the witness collapses and confesses that he is a liar. More likely, he will rise to levels of passion and fluency hitherto unseen.

In cross examination you are allowed to ask leading questions. Indeed, you should try to lead as much as possible to control the narrative. Bear in mind that whoever you are cross-examining is there only because, overall, his evidence is damaging to your client's case. The last thing that you should be doing is giving him scope to provide even more damaging evidence than he has already given in examination in chief.

According to the *Annotated Rules of the Court of Session*, 36.11.2 cross examination is designed "to weaken or destroy the witness' version of facts [not the witness himself!] and to elicit evidence favourable to the cross-examiner."

Note that there are two purposes here; but as regards the second one you may well find that the witness cannot or just will not provide you with any favourable evidence; or you might have to try to weaken or destroy the witness's account so much that it would be inconsistent to ask the court to rely on anything he says at all.

You must put it to a witness that he is incorrect or dishonest if that is necessary but do not flog a dead horse. If the person is adamant, just move on unless you are going to confront him with a prior inconsistent statement or something that might undermine him.

If you are looking to get favourable evidence out of somebody as well as seeking to contradict or challenge him make sure that you get the good evidence before you alienate the witness by criticising him.

There is a third purpose in cross examination. If you intend later to lead evidence to contradict what is being said by the witness whom you are cross examining, you should put that to the witness so that he can comment on it. I have already looked at this in the context of the advantages of leading at proof. Remember that the witness is commenting on evidence only. Do not give him the opportunity to say anything on the submissions that you intend to make to the sheriff.

Another risk attached to failing to cross examine on an important point is that it can result in a reference in the sheriff's judgment to his accepting "the unchallenged evidence" of the opponent's witness.

Unless the evidence was actually indisputable and therefore unchallengeable, this is ammunition for the disgruntled client to make a complaint.

If you ask a witness a question which if answered might incriminate the witness, or amount to an admission of adultery, he does not have to answer it and the sheriff has to warn him that he doesn't have to answer. So, e.g., possession of drugs.

You have to have a basis for putting a proposition to a witness, especially one concerning criminal behaviour. So you could not cross-examine a witness about cocaine use unless his own medical notes had mentioned it. That your own clients had just had a suspicion would not be enough.

Remember that when you are examining or cross-examining witnesses you are in a privileged position. This must be the only job in the world where you can call somebody a liar without getting sued for defamation. But you cannot abuse that privilege and courts will visit their wrath upon you if you do.

The Law Society of Scotland Practice Rules say (B1.13) that "when questioning witnesses treat them with appropriate respect and courtesy". The rules relating to solicitor advocates say (4.4.45) that you must not abuse your position "for example, by bullying or insulting behaviour".

Third parties, including witnesses can, and do, complain to the SLCC. This could happen to any of us. A sheriff principal told me that it had happened to him when he was a practising solicitor. A witness who complains that you called him a liar is likely to be wasting everybody's time if you are acting on instructions and it is a reasonable or necessary stance to take (after all, if you do not challenge an opponent's credibility your own client could complain about you) and you do not do it in a bullying or insulting way. Also, if the opposing solicitor or the sheriff has not intervened its unlikely to be serious enough to succeed as a complaint.

CHAPTER 21

JUDICIAL KNOWLEDGE

You do not need to lead evidence of matters that are within judicial knowledge. This means that you should not waste time or money or taking risks doing so. However, the scope of such knowledge can sometimes be hard to define.

For example, having undertaken hundreds of car accident proofs I have found it to be unnecessary to lead expert opinion evidence as to the inferences to be drawn from damage to vehicles. Sheriffs will use their own knowledge to say that a dent indicates an impact at right angles to the surface whereas a scrape indicates a degree of sideways contact. Having said that, I had a case in Hamilton in 2019 where the sheriff said that he could not draw any inferences from vehicle damage as to how the impact had occurred and that needed expert evidence.

Walkers (11.7) gives examples of facts that are in within judicial knowledge. These are from cases from the 1920s, 1930s and 1940s respectively; "the mischievous habits of children", "the conditions of the local labour market and the average wages of different types of worker" and "the differences between the habits and equipment of legitimate anglers and salmon poachers".

With the exception of the first, it would be foolhardy for an agent now to assume that any of this was within judicial knowledge.

Walkers state that facts should be confined to common knowledge but that common knowledge will vary from one locality to another. Another complication is that it will vary from one sheriff to another too; we now have specialist sheriffs, in personal injury, family and commercial cases.

I have conducted proofs in which the method by which duty is paid on goods stored in a bonded warehouse was held to be within judicial knowledge as were the trading practices of dealers in the wholesale jewellery business. In my view, although these were within the knowledge of the commercial sheriff who heard the proofs they are not within general judicial knowledge.

The obvious problem here is that you do cannot know the ambits of judicial knowledge in a particular case in advance of the commencement of the proof itself, so you cannot fully plan for it. The solicitor is at risk in that he might assume that something is within judicial knowledge, not lead evidence about it and then find that the court holds that it is not.

On the other hand, you could be criticised for needlessly citing witnesses or spending time and money to prove things that the court says are within judicial knowledge. At one time in Glasgow there were child psychologists quite often giving evidence in contact proofs, and as I recall, sheriffs did not approve, and that practice died out.

There is no hard and fast rule here, other than to try to anticipate problems and discuss them with the client; so that the client takes the decision and risk about having witnesses ready to lead evidence.

CHAPTER 22

ORDINARY CAUSE RULES ON RUNNING A PROOF

Read the rules before you become subject to them. There is little point of learning about a time limit after you have exceeded it. The rules may have been amended from when you last looked at them. Given that they are changed often this is quite likely. Also, it is easy to assume that in the sheriff court the rules are always, by default, the Ordinary Cause Rules. But these don't apply to Summary Applications; the Act of Sederunt Summary Applications, Statutory Applications and Appeals etc 1999 applies.

Summary Applications are common. No record of the evidence is made unless the sheriff so orders (1907 Act S50). You need to observe the rules of evidence and principles of civil litigation and natural justice. But from a practical perspective check as early as possible with the court whether the sheriff wants a shorthand writer instructed.

In contested commissary causes which go to proof the Ordinary Cause Rules apply; *Currie* on Confirmation 19-13.

In addition, within the O.C.R.s there are numerous rules that apply only to certain types of case. Family Cases, Commercial Actions and Personal Injury claims are all treated as special kinds of action, with their own rules. Significantly too, the rules governing these types of case are characterised by case management, whereby the sheriff can control what you are to set out to prove and how you are to do it. This can have benefits if we consider the self-preservation factor already mentioned If the sheriff wishes to control the proof it takes some of the responsibility away from you if it goes badly.

CHAPTER 23

THE LAW OF EVIDENCE

Until the Civil Evidence (Scotland) Act 1988 relaxed the rules dramatically, the law of evidence was very arcane. The best evidence rule meant that other forms of evidence were inadmissible, not merely inferior. Hearsay was not admissible except in particular scenarios such as where someone had died. Corroboration was required except in personal injury cases.

Whereas the rules of procedure get more and more convoluted, in practice there are very few rules of evidence left in civil procedure, and a failure to adhere to them is unlikely to be fatal. Instead, it is likely to lead to a discharge or continuation of a proof.

Remember that objections to evidence are made at the time you seek someone seeks to use it, not when it is lodged, for example evidence irregularly obtained. In my experience objections to evidence irregularly obtained are never successful.

Some useful bits of legislation

Section 1 of the 1988 Act abolishes the rule requiring corroboration, so the court may crucial facts proved even if evidence for them derives from only one source.

In effect, there is still an exception in relation to actions of divorce and dissolution of a civil partnership, because that one source has to be somebody other than the parties to the action. So in practice you will find that if everything goes to plan the same evidence is coming from your client and someone else.

So, other than in such cases you do not need to bring a supporting witness to corroborate the evidence of your main witness. Neither do you have to bring as a witness somebody who made a statement if you have a witness to say that he heard the statement made.

However, the 1988 Act concerns admissibility, not weight. It did not say either than corroboration does not matter or that hearsay is as good as direct evidence. Neither of those statements is true.

The abolition of the need for corroboration has misled some into the dangerous belief that it is safe to enter a proof the success of which hinges on establishing key findings in fact where is the only source is the uncorroborated evidence of a witness whose credibility or reliability is in dispute. This could be, for example, a road traffic proof where there were no witnesses other than the two drivers, pursuer and defender. Perilling the whole case on such a pursuer's evidence alone is highly risky. There is a reason why the Scottish Legal Aid Board requires corroboration to be provided with an application for legal aid.

And if you have the ability to corroborate evidence you have to be careful about not doing so. To give an example; in a road traffic case my experience is that if there is a dispute about liability and you do not call a passenger in your client's vehicle it can undermine your client's account (because it begs the question as to why did you not call a witness who is likely to have seen what happened) So if the passenger is absent get an explanation from the client in evidence court; e.g. that the passenger is at school or abroad on holiday.

Another example is in contact cases; If your client is seeking a Section 9 order it always looks better if he has a witness there (e.g. his mother) to say what a wonderful chap he is, even though that evidence might not carry a great deal of weight.

Section 2 of the 1988 Act abolished the rule that hearsay evidence is inadmissible. Hearsay evidence is evidence of what someone else has stated orally or in writing. Before the 1988 Act you were not able to use hearsay evidence of a witness to prove the truth of what was allegedly said by another person who was not a witness. This is called secondary hearsay. But you could use it to prove that something had actually been said by that person (primary hearsay) not whether what had been said was true or not.

The rule against secondary hearsay was because the court could not assess the credibility or reliability of the maker of the statement, because the maker of the statement couldn't be tested by cross examination and because the person giving the hearsay evidence might not have heard or read it correctly. These weaknesses are still true, which is why hearsay is inferior evidence.

Bear in mind that productions can amount to hearsay evidence.

To facilitate the leading of documentary hearsay evidence, you should look at Sections 2(1)(b) and 6 of the 1988 Act.

OCR 29.3 refers to S2(1)(b), which concerns statements "made by a person other than in the course of proof" and it allows you to docquet such a written statement that you want to be received as evidence, where the maker of the statement is not a witness. Similarly, Section 6 of the 1988 Act allows you to lodge authenticated copies of documents.

The interaction of these two provisions of the 1988 Act features in *Japan Leasing (Europe) plc v Weir's Trustee (No 2)* 1998 SLT 973. It seems that S2(1)(b) is designed to cover past statements whereas the documents in *Japan Leasing* were contractual, and should have been authenticated under S6.

This can be a complicated area and in my experience these 1988 provisions are rarely used. Instead, agents nearly always lodge copies and try to get them agreed either in a Minute of Admissions or by a Notice to Admit. If you are going to have to rely on documentary evidence where there will not be a witness to speak to it you need to consider how best to get the evidence in, and look at these sections of the 1988 Act. Do it in plenty of time.

Sections 10–11 of the Law Reform (Miscellaneous Provisions) (Scotland) Act 1968 invert the onus of proof where somebody has a conviction. So if your client's opponent has a conviction for assault the civil court will proceed on the presumption that he did that of which he was convicted, ie he assaulted that complainer. It would be for the presumed assailant to rebut that presumption (on a lower standard of proof, obviously). If you are going to rely on the 1968 Act take steps as early as possible to recover evidence of the conviction, because that can be difficult and time consuming.

Standard of proof

"Balance of probabilities" just means; what probably happened or what is likely to have happened. It is not a high test. The other standard, beyond reasonable doubt, applies in a handful of types of civil action, for example in breach of interdict cases.

Some particular types of proof

Traditionally, affidavits are lodged to avoid the need for someone to attend court. However, in some proofs the witnesses attend and adopt the content of affidavits which they have already given and which have been lodged.

If you are facing a proof conducted this way, which is perfectly competent if a little counter-intuitive, you need to adapt your approach towards cross examination. I have seen this practice in adoption cases, where the local authority lodges the affidavits of witnesses who also turn up. The witnesses are then called and asked to adopt their affidavits, which they do. It takes two minutes. The other party is then immediately put on the back foot in having to cross examine. So make sure that you have read the affidavits carefully and identified the questions you want to put in cross examination beforehand.

Incidentally, on the subject of affidavits, these can be used in any action They are useful in saving money, assuming that the deponent does not also attend as a witness, but they carry risks. You have to warn the client about those risks. There is a trade-off between expense and producing inferior evidence.

<u>Undefended proofs</u>; are rare. I have conducted these only in divorce cases where, in effect, there has to be both evidence and corroboration. If the case is undefended from the start the practice is to lodge affidavits when you are minuting for decree. The cases of mine that reached undefended proof stage were initially defended but either settled or had the Defender throwing in the towel on the day of the proof. The sheriff might have continued the case as undefended for affidavits to be lodged but it was quicker and more convenient just to have an undefended proof there and then. These are easy. You simply ask the witnesses questions mirroring what you would have put in their affidavits.

<u>Expert witnesses.</u> By far the best authority for identifying the role of an expert witness is the Supreme Court case of *Cordia v Kennedy* [2016] UKSC 6.

My view is that it is not a good idea for experts to sit through the evidence of any other witnesses. There is the potential for the expert reaching an interpretation of the factual evidence different from the sheriff's interpretation, and opining on his own interpretation – it is a lot more controlled if the court knows the material or assumed facts on which the expert has based his opinion. There is textbook authority to say that experts can sit through the evidence of other witnesses, but I have found that sheriffs generally disapprove of this practice.

As a safeguard, if your expert has produced a report, lodge it and get the expert to adopt it. Ie ask the witness in the box; "Do you adopt as your evidence the contents of your report" That makes their whole report evidence; so if you take the expert through the report but forget to ask him something about it you can legitimately say in your submissions that the whole of the report constitutes evidence.

CHAPTER 24

RUNNING A HOPELESS PROOF

The ending of a battle against overwhelming odds is more likely to resemble a Little Bighorn than a Rorke's Drift. Generally, if you do not think that there is a realistic prospect of success you should be advising the client not to proceed to proof, and if the client wants to proceed anyway (as is his right) he needs to be warned about expenses, including the danger of these being on the agent-client scale if the sheriff feels that there has been flagrant timewasting and stubbornness tantamount to an abuse of process. However, in family cases the courts take a far more nuanced approach to take account of natural instincts and affinities.

I acted for a mother with a chaotic lifestyle, including hard drug use, who opposed the adoption of her daughter by her very respectable former husband and his new equally respectable wife. I acted for a father with a serious drink problem who was seeking contact to his 15-year old son. The son did not want to see his father and he had made his wishes clear both to his *curator ad litem* and to the child welfare reporter.

Both these clients were unsuccessful. The chances of success were always virtually zero, but these two parents wanted their child to know that they had tried to maintain contact. And although the court refused, the clients at least had the consolation that they had tried. It would require a heart of stone to condemn them for that.

The most important thing here is managing clients' expectations. In other words letting them know that they are almost certainly bound to lose.

CHAPTER 25

IF THE PROOF IS LOST

The "no win no fee" or success fee agreement culture is a wonderful notion where a client has been hit by a car whilst using a pedestrian crossing and the lawyer's job is simply to obtain as high an award of damages as possible, with an abundance of expenses on top. In plenty of other types of case this doctrine is a source of trouble, engendering an ugly corollary whereby some clients suppose that if they lose their case their lawyer should take a lesser fee or none at all.

It is as spurious to suppose that lawyers who act in easy cases win them through skill and talent as it is to assume that those who act in difficult ones are to blame when they are lost.

Statistically, as many proofs are lost as won, just as for every Yan there is a Ying. Over the many hundreds of proofs that I have undertaken I have probably encountered failure more often than success. So as long as you have done your best never blame yourself, but learn from the experience and move on.

Never tell a client that you have lost a proof, or even that "we" have lost. Distance yourself personally and say that the proof was lost. Deflect focus away from yourself.

Always advise in relation to an appeal. Make sure that you do it in plenty of time and give the client the choice; make it his decision, not yours. Remember that if the appeal is in relation to the evidence you will need the extension of the shorthand notes and, as has been mentioned above, these can be very expensive.

Some clients think that an appeal is a chance to have a re-hearing in front of a different judge, offering the opportunity for a different outcome. If that were so the Sheriff Appeal Court would be inundated by unsuccessful litigants. Instead, clients must be told, before the proof has even occurred, that the cherry may be bitten only once. Appeals are where a sheriff has plainly gone wrong and, crucially, where the outcome would have been different if he had not. There is little point in appealing if the S.A.C. is likely to uphold the same result on a different basis.

CHAPTER 26

CONCLUSION

It has not been the intention of this book to deter you conducting proofs by over-emphasising the hazards. Sometimes it is the only reasonable course open to your client. Running a proof can be enjoyable, but you will find it more so if you have prepared it well, you are properly funded, and you are as well organised as you can be.

BIBLIOGRAPHY

Macphail on Sheriff Court Practice (4th edition, 2022)

Walker and Walker; The Law of Evidence in Scotland

Greens Annotated Rules of the Court of Session; is a great source of information not just about Court of Session procedure but about the sheriff court too, because the annotations include case law and authorities which applies to both courts. So, for example, if you want to check the law on caution for expenses there will be annotations about that. This publication is also up to date, unlike textbooks, which rapidly go out of date.

The Law Society of Scotland Practice Rules 2011

To this bibliography is added the caveat that whilst textbooks are useful in illustrating principles one should never rely on them to explain procedure. To be up to date you need to look at the rules of court themselves.

MORE BOOKS BY LAW BRIEF PUBLISHING

A selection of our other titles available now:-

'A Practical Guide to Estate Administration and Crypto Assets' by Richard Marshall
'A Practical Guide to Managing GDPR Data Subject Access Requests – Second Edition' by Patrick O'Kane
'A Practical Guide to Parental Alienation in Private and Public Law Children Cases' by Sam King QC & Frankie Shama
'Contested Heritage – Removing Art from Land and Historic Buildings' by Richard Harwood QC, Catherine Dobson, David Sawtell
'The Limits of Separate Legal Personality: When Those Running a Company Can Be Held Personally Liable for Losses Caused to Third Parties Outside of the Company' by Dr Mike Wilkinson
'A Practical Guide to Transgender Law' by Robin Moira White & Nicola Newbegin
'A Practical Guide to 'Stranded Spouses' in Family Law' by Mani Singh Basi
'A Practical Guide to Residential Freehold Conveyancing' by Lorraine Richardson
'A Practical Guide to Pensions on Divorce for Lawyers' by Bryan Scant
'A Practical Guide to Challenging Sham Marriage Allegations in Immigration Law' by Priya Solanki
'A Practical Guide to Legal Rights in Scotland' by Sarah-Jane Macdonald
'A Practical Guide to New Build Conveyancing' by Paul Sams & Rebecca East
'A Practical Guide to Defending Barristers in Disciplinary Cases' by Marc Beaumont
'A Practical Guide to Inherited Wealth on Divorce' by Hayley Trim
'A Practical Guide to Practice Direction 12J and Domestic Abuse in Private Law Children Proceedings' by Rebecca Cross & Malvika Jaganmohan
'A Practical Guide to Confiscation and Restraint' by Narita Bahra QC, John Carl Townsend, David Winch
'A Practical Guide to the Law of Forests in Scotland' by Philip Buchan
'A Practical Guide to Health and Medical Cases in Immigration Law' by Rebecca Chapman & Miranda Butler

'A Practical Guide to Bad Character Evidence for Criminal Practitioners by Aparna Rao
'A Practical Guide to Extradition Law post-Brexit' by Myles Grandison et al
'A Practical Guide to Hoarding and Mental Health for Housing Lawyers' by Rachel Coyle
'A Practical Guide to Psychiatric Claims in Personal Injury – 2nd Edition' by Liam Ryan
'Stephens on Contractual Indemnities' by Richard Stephens
'A Practical Guide to the EU Succession Regulation' by Richard Frimston
'A Practical Guide to Solicitor and Client Costs – 2nd Edition' by Robin Dunne
'Constructive Dismissal – Practice Pointers and Principles' by Benjimin Burgher
'A Practical Guide to Religion and Belief Discrimination Claims in the Workplace' by Kashif Ali
'A Practical Guide to the Law of Medical Treatment Decisions' by Ben Troke
'Fundamental Dishonesty and QOCS in Personal Injury Proceedings: Law and Practice' by Jake Rowley
'A Practical Guide to the Law in Relation to School Exclusions' by Charlotte Hadfield & Alice de Coverley
'A Practical Guide to Divorce for the Silver Separators' by Karin Walker
'The Right to be Forgotten – The Law and Practical Issues' by Melissa Stock
'A Practical Guide to Planning Law and Rights of Way in National Parks, the Broads and AONBs' by James Maurici QC, James Neill et al
'A Practical Guide to Election Law' by Tom Tabori
'A Practical Guide to the Law in Relation to Surrogacy' by Andrew Powell
'A Practical Guide to Claims Arising from Fatal Accidents – 2nd Edition' by James Patience
'A Practical Guide to the Ownership of Employee Inventions – From Entitlement to Compensation' by James Tumbridge & Ashley Roughton
'A Practical Guide to Asbestos Claims' by Jonathan Owen & Gareth McAloon
'A Practical Guide to Stamp Duty Land Tax in England and Northern Ireland' by Suzanne O'Hara
'A Practical Guide to the Law of Farming Partnerships' by Philip Whitcomb
'Covid-19, Homeworking and the Law – The Essential Guide to Employment and GDPR Issues' by Forbes Solicitors
'Covid-19 and Criminal Law – The Essential Guide' by Ramya Nagesh

'Covid-19 and Family Law in England and Wales – The Essential Guide' by Safda Mahmood
'A Practical Guide to the Law of Unlawful Eviction and Harassment – 2nd Edition' by Stephanie Lovegrove
'Covid-19, Brexit and the Law of Commercial Leases – The Essential Guide' by Mark Shelton
'A Practical Guide to Costs in Personal Injury Claims – 2nd Edition' by Matthew Hoe
'A Practical Guide to the General Data Protection Regulation (GDPR) – 2nd Edition' by Keith Markham
'Ellis on Credit Hire – Sixth Edition' by Aidan Ellis & Tim Kevan
'A Practical Guide to Working with Litigants in Person and McKenzie Friends in Family Cases' by Stuart Barlow
'Protecting Unregistered Brands: A Practical Guide to the Law of Passing Off' by Lorna Brazell
'A Practical Guide to Secondary Liability and Joint Enterprise Post-Jogee' by Joanne Cecil & James Mehigan
'A Practical Guide to the Pre-Action RTA Claims Protocol for Personal Injury Lawyers' by Antonia Ford
'A Practical Guide to Neighbour Disputes and the Law' by Alexander Walsh
'A Practical Guide to Forfeiture of Leases' by Mark Shelton
'A Practical Guide to Coercive Control for Legal Practitioners and Victims' by Rachel Horman
'Tackling Disclosure in the Criminal Courts – A Practitioner's Guide' by Narita Bahra QC & Don Ramble
'A Practical Guide to the Law of Driverless Cars – Second Edition' by Alex Glassbrook, Emma Northey & Scarlett Milligan
'A Practical Guide to TOLATA Claims' by Greg Williams
'A Practical Guide to Elderly Law – 2nd Edition' by Justin Patten
'A Practical Guide to Responding to Housing Disrepair and Unfitness Claims' by Iain Wightwick
'A Practical Guide to the Law of Bullying and Harassment in the Workplace' by Philip Hyland
'How to Be a Freelance Solicitor: A Practical Guide to the SRA-Regulated Freelance Solicitor Model' by Paul Bennett
'A Practical Guide to Prison Injury Claims' by Malcolm Johnson

'A Practical Guide to the Small Claims Track – 2nd Edition' by Dominic Bright
'A Practical Guide to Advising Clients at the Police Station' by Colin Stephen McKeown-Beaumont
'A Practical Guide to Antisocial Behaviour Injunctions' by Iain Wightwick
'Practical Mediation: A Guide for Mediators, Advocates, Advisers, Lawyers, and Students in Civil, Commercial, Business, Property, Workplace, and Employment Cases' by Jonathan Dingle with John Sephton
'The Mini-Pupillage Workbook' by David Boyle
'A Practical Guide to Crofting Law' by Brian Inkster
'A Practical Guide to the Law of Domain Names and Cybersquatting' by Andrew Clemson
'A Practical Guide to the Law of Gender Pay Gap Reporting' by Harini Iyengar
'NHS Whistleblowing and the Law' by Joseph England
'Employment Law and the Gig Economy' by Nigel Mackay & Annie Powell
'A Practical Guide to Noise Induced Hearing Loss (NIHL) Claims' by Andrew Mckie, Ian Skeate, Gareth McAloon
'An Introduction to Beauty Negligence Claims – A Practical Guide for the Personal Injury Practitioner' by Greg Almond
'Intercompany Agreements for Transfer Pricing Compliance' by Paul Sutton
'Zen and the Art of Mediation' by Martin Plowman
'A Practical Guide to the SRA Principles, Individual and Law Firm Codes of Conduct 2019 – What Every Law Firm Needs to Know' by Paul Bennett
'A Practical Guide to Adoption for Family Lawyers' by Graham Pegg
'A Practical Guide to Industrial Disease Claims' by Andrew Mckie & Ian Skeate
'A Practical Guide to Redundancy' by Philip Hyland
'A Practical Guide to Vicarious Liability' by Mariel Irvine
'A Practical Guide to Applications for Landlord's Consent and Variation of Leases' by Mark Shelton
'A Practical Guide to Relief from Sanctions Post-Mitchell and Denton' by Peter Causton
'A Practical Guide to Equity Release for Advisors' by Paul Sams
'A Practical Guide to Financial Services Claims' by Chris Hegarty
'The Law of Houses in Multiple Occupation: A Practical Guide to HMO Proceedings' by Julian Hunt

'Occupiers, Highways and Defective Premises Claims: A Practical Guide Post-Jackson – 2nd Edition' by Andrew Mckie
'A Practical Guide to Financial Ombudsman Service Claims' by Adam Temple & Robert Scrivenor
'A Practical Guide to Running Housing Disrepair and Cavity Wall Claims: 2nd Edition' by Andrew Mckie & Ian Skeate
'A Practical Guide to Holiday Sickness Claims – 2nd Edition' by Andrew Mckie & Ian Skeate
'Arguments and Tactics for Personal Injury and Clinical Negligence Claims' by Dorian Williams
'A Practical Guide to Drone Law' by Rufus Ballaster, Andrew Firman, Eleanor Clot
'A Practical Guide to Compliance for Personal Injury Firms Working With Claims Management Companies' by Paul Bennett
'RTA Allegations of Fraud in a Post-Jackson Era: The Handbook – 2nd Edition' by Andrew Mckie
'RTA Personal Injury Claims: A Practical Guide Post-Jackson' by Andrew Mckie
'On Experts: CPR35 for Lawyers and Experts' by David Boyle
'An Introduction to Personal Injury Law' by David Boyle

www.ingramcontent.com/pod-product-compliance
Lightning Source LLC
LaVergne TN
LVHW022108200926
848481LV00003B/1098
* 9 7 8 1 9 1 6 6 9 8 2 5 3 *